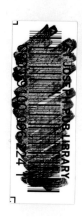

CANVAS AND ROPE CRAFT

CANVAS
AND ROPE CRAFT

FOR THE PRACTICAL BOATOWNER

Frank Rosenow

W · W · NORTON & COMPANY
New York   London

Published simultaneously in Canada by Penguin Books
Canada Ltd., 2801 John Street, Markham, Ontario L3R 1B4.

Printed in the United States of America.

Library of Congress Cataloging-in-Publication Data
Rosenow, Frank, 1944-
Canvas and rope craft for the practical boatowner.
1. Marine canvas work. 2. Knots and splices.
I. Title.
VM531.R66 1987   623.8'62   88–5127

ISBN 0-393-03322-8

W. W. Norton & Company, Inc., 500 Fifth Avenue,
New York, N.Y. 10110
W. W. Norton & Company Ltd., 37 Great Russell Street,
London WC1B 3NU

1 2 3 4 5 6 7 8 9 0

*To amass wealth by the million does not compare
with the mastery of a small skill*

Chinese proverb

FISHERMAN'S
WHIPPING
(PELOPONNESUS)

Contents

Introduction: the right way

At a second-hand bookseller's in London's Charing Cross Road, I recently spent seventy-five pence on a cardboard-bound octavo volume called *The Right Way to do House Repairs*. On the frayed jacket, the publisher assures the reader that every title on his list (*The Right Way to Ride a Horse, To become a Successful Shop Assistant* etc.) is written by an expert 'so the cultured layman who wishes to study any subject can do so with complete confidence'.

His message carries the conviction that there is a Right Way to Paint a Wall or to Repair a WC Cistern.

As a sailmaker's apprentice on the west coast of Sweden I was once trained to hold a similar view about canvas work. The master sailmaker did things The Right Way and as an apprentice you strove to come close to his supposed perfection in cutting a sail or striking out the curves of a boatcover on canvas.

My mentor, Herr Andersson, loved to tell me about his own apprentice days early in the century. Then, he said, the fledgling had to buy his master a dram before he was shown something that required particular sleight of hand. Herr Andersson himself, a fine and generous man, had me pull my workbench close to his and showed me how to lay a hand to canvas for no consideration at all.

As my work in the loft progressed logically from a simple canvas bag, to a set of lifeboat sails, to square sails for a Greek school ship, there came a gradual assurance. This book is structured in a similar way, project by project.

Yet, the hand skills I first developed were bound up with a spacious and level loft floor, a large canvas inventory and several sewing machines for different grades of cloth.

Since then, a journey south has made for a more advanced outlook. The vehicle was a sailing boat called the *Moth*. She was laid up in fibreglass on the west coast of Sweden before I took her to a finishing yard at the northern end of the Vänern lake to complete the interior.

On launching, her canvas inventory was a 5½ oz mainsail and a self-tacking jib in 4½ oz Dacron, plus an acrylic canvas sprayhood with transparent plastic windows sewn in.

The sails set fair and well, except that the roach of the mainsail was too big. Every time the boat came about a short portion of the leech touched the backstay. Many moons later, approaching the island of Tinos in the Cyclades with downdrafts at 10 Beaufort, the mainsail within seconds disintegrated into the separate parts that had once been on the sailmaker's floor. The first thing that went was the leech tabling, then the seams in every panel sprang up, starting at the outside end.

From Vänern, I set sail south and my reality began to change. At Vedbaek in Denmark I sailed in to see the sailmaking Carlsen brothers. They sold me materials for a light genoa which I finished on the dock, by hand.

Two months later the *Moth* sailed into Alicante on the Spanish Costa Blanca. With Christmas approaching, there were 80 foreign cruising yachts tied stern or bow-to the palm-lined promenade. We ranged in size from the 18 ft hard-chine plywood sloop *Oltre L'Orizzonte* from Viareggio in Italy to the 65 ft *Ferrossimo* from Brussels. My neighbour on one side was the 38 ft 'Joshua' design ketch *Übu* from Bretagne. Claude and Paquita Laborde had made a good job of their home project, crowning her indigo, seamanlike sheer with tall, laminated spruce spars. They were busy topside, making a bright blue sprayhood from the same ribbed rubber fabric that is used in the soft roll-top of the Citroen 2CV. The sewing machine was on loan from another triple-chiner, the hole punch came from the *Moth* and the die and eyelets from the pride of our community, a magnificently baggy-wrinkled British Colin Archer.

The atmosphere was contagious. I located a bolt of light canvas ashore and began to make a sail cover on the deck of the motor yacht *Saphir*, belonging to an obliging undertaker's florist from Cologne.

I would have been better off doing preventive maintenance. A few months later, in the gusty Straights of Bonifacio, between Corsica and Sardinia, the swept back spreaders poked a hole through the mainsail.

In the placid lagoon of Porto Cervo on the Costa Smeralda I attended to the patch and admired the canvaswork on display along the docks. For instance on the venerable Honduras mahogany ketch *Erna of Fairlee*, secure in her berth below the Scacco Matto bluff at the harbour entrance, the cushions by the brass-studded mahogany wheel were as powder blue as ever I have seen. The snow white sail covers came off only for scrubbing.

At the toe end of Italy, en route for Yugoslavia, I went into the Standa supermarket at Brindisi and bought a 'Percale Matrimoniale' in royal blue cotton. The double-bed sheet was already hemmed so all I had to do to make it shipshape was to hand sew four clew patches to the corners and punch four No.1 eyelets in. Throughout a hot summer's sailing between dry Yugoslav islets, the 'Matrimoniale' set beautifully over the cockpit, the tension wrinkles totally contained by the cotton corner patches and the blue colour taking the edge off the sun.

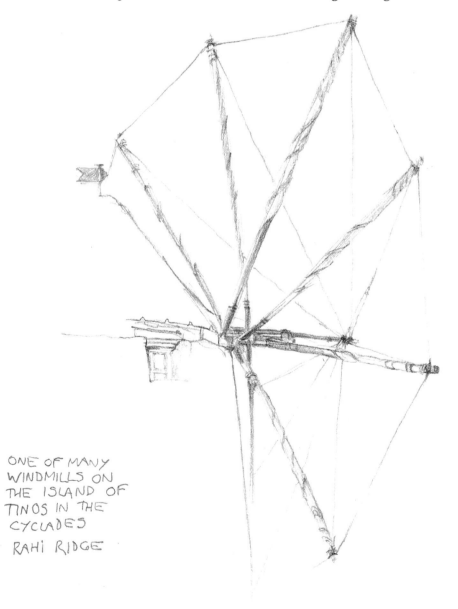

ONE OF MANY
WINDMILLS ON
THE ISLAND OF
TINOS IN THE
CYCLADES
RAHI RIDGE

The mainsail blowout in the Cyclades kept me busy flatseaming everything back together again on the Tinos quay, although I did make an excursion up to the ever-windswept mountain ridge by Rahi which was red with blooming heather.

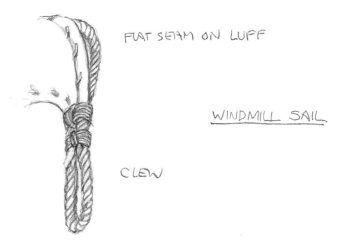

FLAT SEAM ON LUFF

WINDMILL SAIL

CLEW

There was a windmill there, facing north from where the wind blew strong and full. Its wings were fashioned like the spars of a clipper, doubled where they joined and where the strain was greatest. Quarter-inch iron rods bound one wing tip to the next, and from the ends there also ran a brace of wires to the end of a central spar that ranged out in front like a bowsprit.

Hemp ropes ran along the running-stitched cotton sails which could be roller-reefed. Details, like the sail clews, were unconventional in sailmaking terms, but simple and adequate.

THE REFURBISHED MAINSAIL AS SEEN ON DEPARTURE FROM TINOS

Back on the water, the born-again mainsail set very well, in spite of a crazy zig-zag leech.

At length I came to Turkey. In Kuşadasi, on the Söke road, there was a man who sold tolerable cotton canvas very cheaply. When I requested a bolt, he offered to sew me a new set of cushions from it for an extra few dollars. I agreed, curious to see his style of work. My light blue factory bunk covers were backed with black nylon which had not been properly hemmed or heatsealed and kept snagging the cheap nylon zippers. The Turkish cotton covers were made without any zipper closure. Instead, the backing side was made in two pieces, overlapping one another. The cushion was simply slipped into the aperture in between. I knew the arrangement only from pillows.

Similarly, sun awnings made by the only sailmaker in Bodrum did not have spur teeth grommets along the edge to take the lanyards, but the lanyards themselves were sewn to the tabling. As a cruising friend, David Edwards of Venice, California, found out, sails proper were less agreeably simplified. He ordered a new cat sail for his dinghy and it was delivered with batten pockets that stopped two inches short of the leech, causing the roach to make an infernal clatter.

In Fethiye, further south, there was a man who did know what he was about. Methin Balaban's business was to make quilted vests for mopeds, principally French Mobylettes which have long been made under licence in Turkey. The vests of Methin Balaban were not for warmth but they served a purpose. In every one of them was an ornate pocket which contained a match-box size edition of the Koran.

Methin also made seat covers, cutting to size with a wonderfully sure eye without templates. As with the vests, the fasteners were soft cotton string that stretched just enough to keep a cover in place under use.

He also knew something about style. While his many competitors offered every combination of bright red, yellow, green and blue vinyl, a quilted Balaban vest could be distinguished among thousands by the exclusive use of a red, black and white colour combination. When I reached Myra, on the south coast of Turkey, the Balaban colours and basic patterns appeared again in the mosaics in the 600 AD crypt of the church of St Nicholas of Myra, protector of children and sailors.

On the Nile river, where the weaving of cotton cloth began, long ago, things are done as in Looking-glass Land, back to front. Early one morning I found Akasha Mohammed Mahmud down by the sandy river bank at Luxor. He began to lay out a new felucca sail on a level, sheltered piece of ground at the water's edge. With no outline drawn, he laid down panel by panel, squinting hard with his one good eye as he cut them to size. The cotton was a coarse local weave. It was light on his hands as he began to ply the needle and unlikely to mildew in the dry and windy conditions of the upper Nile.

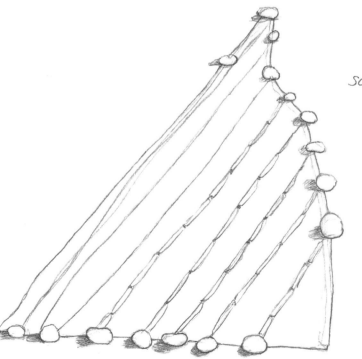

FELUCCA SAIL

SCOOPED OUTLINE SHAPE

STOPS BETWEEN PANELS AT
HALF METER INTERVALS

FIRST FIVE PANELS FULL WIDTH (90 CM)

REMAINING PANELS OUT TO LEECH
RIPPED UP TO HALF WIDTH AND
SEWED IN NARROW PANELS

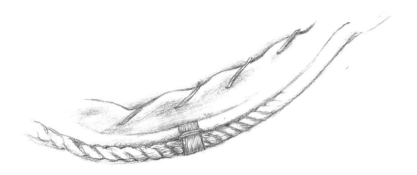

SAIL TABLING AT LUFF (IT IS THE SAME ON THE FOOT)
LATEEN-RIGGED FELUCCA
LUXOR, EGYPT

TWINE: DOUBLED COTTON FOR SEWING

LUFF ROPE: ONE COTTON
LUFF ROPE SEWN INTO ONE-INCH
TABLING, ANOTHER SEIZED TO THE
FIRST AS SHOWN AT DISTANCE
EQUALLING THE DISTANCE
BETWEEN THE SAILMAKER'S THUMB
AND LITTLE FINGER WHEN HIS
HAND IS FULLY SPREAD.

CLOTH: MUCH RESEMBLES GOOD
COTTON SACK MATERIAL.

A little later, he instructed his boat boy Ahmed and a few other youngsters who were loitering on the bank to sew up the sail panels with doubled lengths of cotton twine knotted overhand at the end. Squatting like tailors, they set to work with short darning needles, making a round selvedge-to-selvedge seam. Mahmud fetched a tin of red lead paint to better the watchful eyes of the falcon Horas that gazed from the bow of his boat, the *Onass*. Easily, he traced in the Arabic characters from right to left and watched as I, equally easily, traced in the adjacent Roman letters from left to right.

Later still, we went out on the river, breaking the sail out from along the mast rather than hoisting it, gybing with the boom or lower spar two-blocked against the mast rather than vanged down and reefing by lacing up the sail on the upper spar rather than reefing along the foot. Everything worked just as well as if it had been done 'Right'.

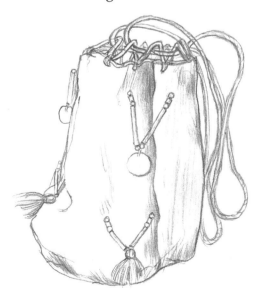

RED-TUFTED, GOLD-SPANGLED
BLACK CLOTH BAG. MAUVE LINING.
TWISTED WOOL LANYARD

BEERSHEBA

13

Sailing to the coast of Israel, I went overland to Beersheba in the Negev desert and came full circle.

In the bedouin market, next to the lambs and goats, the most attractive things were the woven handicrafts in black and primary colours, chiefly red. A stock item was black silk bags, a little smaller than ditty bags, decorated with red tufts of yarn and red embroidery on the bottom. They had no grommets on the upper tabling but a slender bolt rope made of twisted yarns lay around the opening, fastened at regular intervals to allow a yarn lanyard to pass through and pull the bags shut. They were not bags that Herr Andersson would have you make, but they finally made me see how free one can be. And yet, had it not been for the set projects, I would not have been able to appreciate them at all.

The Right Way is your own.

1
Hand seaming

If every man has a vocation, I love hand seaming above all other work. The split second aim before you enter a sharp needle in canvas, the controlled flow of a beeswaxed fathom of twine at every flick of your wrist, and the twack of the line as you heave home on a stitch; there is an exquisite harmony in those things.

As an apprentice I was first set to make a cotton duck seabag with as many seams in it as possible, for practice. The Master, on the next bench along (the traditional sail seaming man was loath to leave his bench and Herr Andersson had both lunch and tea remaining on his bench cushion), watched me thread the needle and run the doubled, twisted thread over a lump of beeswax.

'A flat seam will look neat,' he suggested. 'Right to left, three stitches per inch.'

A little shakily, I began. After a few yards of seaming, and after I had been told to fix the base of the needle in the seaming palm indentation with the tip of my ring finger before taking a stitch, I began to catch the rhythm of the work. You poise the needle with the sharp end almost touching the canvas; push it in with a slight lift of your right hand while your left braces the canvas against the thrust; pull the needle through and take up the slack in the twine with your middle finger – then poise the needle again . . . it is like playing a sprightly little tune over and over. The charm lies in the attempt to perfect the elusive melody. If the stitch is accurately spaced, the timing of pulling the slack twine is sure to be a little out or vice versa.

'It will even out after a few more miles,' said Herr Andersson kindly as I tried to pick up perfect timing. Yet, you never quite do, and therein lies the never-ending challenge of seaming by hand.

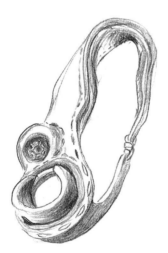

ROPING PALM
FOR HAND SEAMING

In cruising, years after those sailmaking days, handseaming has become the handiest tool of canvas maintenance and replacement.

The sails on my small sloop stay together by virtue of regular inspection and a few timely stitches wherever chafe has parted the original zig-zag machine stitch. Lines and cordage never fray from the end when there is a sewn whipping and, should a pair of dungarees need mending, a sail twine stitch will outlast the material.

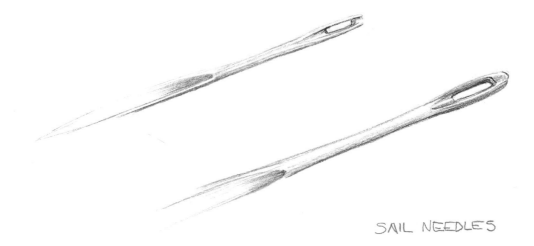

SAIL NEEDLES

In sail maintenance, you are facing a material, Dacron, which will often have a brittle and hard feel, hardly as inviting to a handstitch as the flax or cotton of yore. And yet, with a sharp and unblemished needle, matched to pliable twine that does not stop the needle when it has been pushed through as far as the eye, a few yards of hand seaming is still a joy. If you can utilise the existing machine stitch holes when replacing torn seams, do. The fewer and smaller the holes the better for the strength of the sail.

If a light genoa or dinghy sail needs stitching repair underway or dockside, use the finest triangular section hand seaming needle you can find – hopefully a No.18 – and thread it with a fathom of heavy sewing machine thread that should be twisted and pulled over a lump of beeswax before use. A thread made up from 50 per cent cotton and 50 per cent polyester combines the feel of cotton with the strength of polyester.

If it is difficult to find a seaming needle small enough for the machine thread, use an ordinary sewing needle but try to locate a magnum one, 2½ in (6½ cm) long to fit into the seaming palm.

For heavier work in cotton canvas or Dacron, use larger sail seaming needle. They are numbered from 4 to 18 in the standard Wire Gauge (measuring the round shank of the needle). Four is the largest size, 6 in long.

My own shipboard inventory starts with a No.8 which is useful in guiding the cord in fancy knotting and as a 'bodkin' to work drawstrings or elastic into a tabling. Most use is seen by the 14 to 18 lot and the Wm Smith & Son envelope with five needles, numbered from 14 to 18, is a good first buy.

For a single needle for medium work, a 15 serves.

Pre-waxed nylon or polyester seaming twine used by sailmakers for general hand seaming work is usually of the flat variety, while chandlers prefer to offer small flat spools of round lay stuff such as the No.4 (medium) or No.2 (fine) Marlow whipping twine. For heavy duty hand seaming, the sailmakers twine is robust and practical to work with so try to buy a spool of three ply, 4 oz, from your sailmaker or supplier.

I used to keep my needles in an empty tobacco tin smeared with vaseline but when the *Moth* passed through the canals of France an American friend donated a plastic throat-lozenge box. Some vaseline – petroleum jelly – inside keeps the needles from rattling about and spoiling the points and is good preventive medicine against rust which quickly destroys a needle's usefulness.

To push the needle through the canvas you need a leather palm. There are seaming palms with a metal plate with indentations designed to accept small and medium headed needles, and there are roping palms with larger indentations for all size needles. Sailmakers almost always use roping palms which have a raised

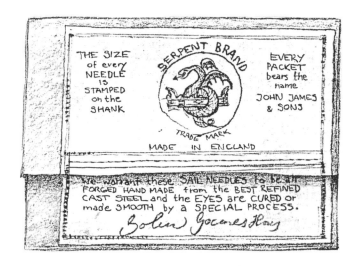

leather thumb guard around which you can wind the twine to heave home on a stitch.

The most prominent maker of palms, Wm Smith & Son, in Beoley Road, Redditch, England, used to supply their line by mail order if requested. Your chandler may also have a good palm in stock but beware of cheap, unstable ones.

In London, Davey & Co, at 5 Grenade Street in the Docklands area, have a good stock of Smith roping palms, ranging from a very satisfactory 'store quality' for nearly £5 to a 'best' sailmaker pattern for nearly £15.

On board the *Moth*, the canvas-piercing hook that is invariably used in loft work on a bench to give equal tension to the cloths sewn sees little use. The bench hook belongs to a bench; on a boat you tend to tension the canvas with a knee or elbow.

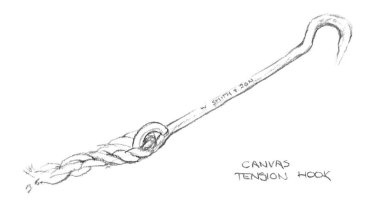

CANVAS TENSION HOOK

The low (15 in [38 cm] for a 6-foot tall canvas worker), 6-foot long backless seaming bench is the best place to hand sew however, so it pays to look for a low stool or other substitute that resembles it in height at least. When possible, I work on the dock sitting on a collapsible, backless Turkish camping stool.

TWISTING ON
A NEW LENGTH
OF TWINE

As you prepare to start seaming, the pre-waxed label on the spool of twine should not prevent you from drawing the doubled, twisted fathom of twine over the best, golden-coloured beeswax you can find. The wax keeps the twist locked in and by softening makes the double twine supple and manageable for seaming.

Thread a fathom of twine and double and wax it before starting work. Mostly, a flat seam is called for in sail repair. As sail panels overlap where they join, a 'double flat seam' is taken, meaning a single flat seam taken from first one and then the other side of the sail.

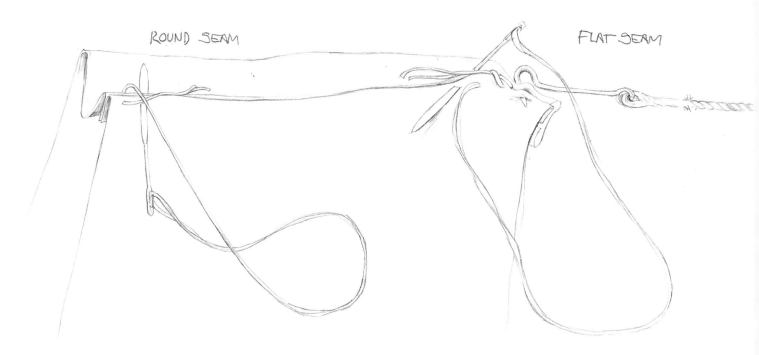

ROUND SEAM

FLAT SEAM

There are, of course, other ways of doing it. A Bremerhaven yachtsman I saw in the Greek port was busy passing a needle through his mainsail to his wife on the other side who in turn passed it back as they chatted away as the one on the blind side tried to keep his fingers away from where he anticipated the next stitch to come through.

When you begin the flat seaming work, make sure the end of the doubled thread is secured under the first few stitches, as shown in the drawing.

If the length of twine runs out, cut it with a good inch to spare. Thread up and wax a new length and twist the end up with the old twine before sewing both ends in as the work is continued.

As the flat seam is taken, from right to left, diagonally across your lap, it helps to have a sail hook with a lanyard fastened to your right and attached to the workpiece. The hook tensions the canvas against the stitches passed. To finish a seam, double back a couple of stitches and tuck the needle under a few stitches for the last pass before cutting the thread.

To reinforce a seam further, you can double back all the way.

In addition to the flat seam is the round seam, which is particularly useful when joining non-fraying edges of cloth. It is passed from left to right.

Whatever stitches you pass, the best way to cultivate a well spaced, seamanlike row of them is to begin with some yards of cotton duck work. A sail seaming bag to keep your palm, twine and needles in will make a good start.

2

Machine sewing

There need be no conflict between hand and machine sewing.

Hand seaming has the advantage, when cruising or racing at sea, of needing the simplest of tools. When applied to a machine-stitched sail it still offers a quick and exceptionally strong way of edge stitching a clew or seizing on piston hanks.

For joining sail panels, tabling a sail cover or making a smooth sail repair patch in Dacron, it would be foolish to argue against the virtues of a sewing machine.

What kind of machine can handle sail and canvas?

To find an answer, I must go back to a Singer Portable Electric (Model No.221-1) which I bought in 1974 at a store called 'Jewellry N' Things' in San Francisco. A slender little fellow from 1932, the machine is popularly known as the Singer Featherweight.

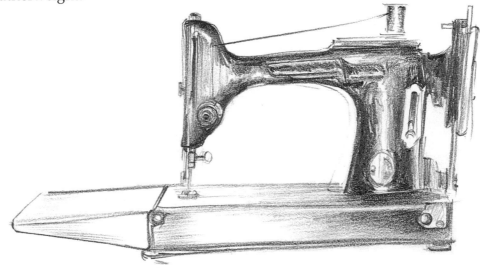

SINGER PORTABLE ELECTRIC 221-1
"FEATHERWEIGHT"

Repairing to my quarters, I immediately set about making a tote bag in 10 oz canvas. Ticking bravely through six layers of cloth, the machine proved strong, reliable and handy. And so it has remained through many heavy bouts of canvaswork.

The straight seam only feature has not been a hindrance in general canvaswork but would have been had I attempted sail seaming with it.

For sails and heavy duty canvaswork on board the *Moth*, I use an Adler-Riccar 260 from the 1960s which, like the Singer, came complete with pristine instruction book and lace ruffling attachment, bearing all the marks of moderate use in the hands of a little old lady. It features zig-zag as well as a straight stitch.

The Adler resembles what in sailing circles is better known as the Read's 'Sailmaker' machine in all things, from the colour of the Feed Dog Adjustment buttons to the thickness of the cast iron body. It even weighs the same 42 lbs (19.1 kg).

It cost the equivalent of $60 compared to the $750 of my last quote for a Reads from Cook Marine Products at Rowayton, Connecticut.

When I blew off the top of my light genoa coming into the Yugoslavian island of Korcula, unwisely holding on to the sail when trying to pass through a National Cruising association flotilla charter group under prudent working sail, Cheryl, the flotilla leader, kindly lent me the NCA's brand new Reads to stitch the top back on. It is a good machine, but not essentially different from what you can pick up much more cheaply secondhand.

The strongest feature on the Reads for cruising folk is the hand crank attachment which is rare on zig-zag machines. There are Russian machines (sold in Greece, I noticed) that have the same combination but the general quality is poor.

Pfaff is a good brand to look for, especially the old 210 model. Beware of Singers with the ancient, shuttlecock lower bobbin as they are difficult to adjust.

Your choice will depend on use. A hand-cranked machine can be a boon in remote areas but most people will be touching civilization fairly often and one can catch up on one's sewing then. For overseas cruising, it is essential to have an adaptor to convert, for instance the 110V American current engine to the European 220.

Survey a used machine carefully, running it threaded on canvas and unthreaded at high revs, listening for odd mechanical sounds. The best guide to its condition is often the outside appearance of its body, carrying case and accessories.

A solid flywheel and heavy iron casting are favourable indicators too.

Try six or eight layers of 12 oz canvas with zig-zag and straight seam, noting how easily the machine handles it, and the amount of space available under the presser foot.

Above all, look for simplicity. Any feature or attachment beyond adjustable straight and zig-zag seams; thread, presser foot and feed tension; and a reverse button, is superfluous for on board or dockside canvas work.

A simple machine needs only simple maintenance. A single drop of sewing machine oil at the juncture of any moving parts is a due that should be paid before use. Where there are interlocking cog wheels, use a paste-consistency sewing machine lubricant. If the machine has been idle a long time, put kerosene in the oiling places, run it, then oil it again.

Make sure the motor drive belt is in good condition and under just enough tension to keep it from slipping.

The bobbin winder belt may also need replacement to work properly. Both are items that should be remembered in the spares satchel.

Other accessories that will be needed are half a dozen bobbins, spare springs for the thread tension and a collection of needles.

For clothes, sail and canvas, I use needles in the 80 to 120 size (also known as 12 to 20 size needles under the other scale of reckoning). The No.90 all-rounder is the best. A batch of special needles for chamois and cowhide have also proved their worth.

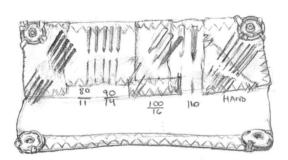

The best thread is a fifty/fifty blend of cotton and polyester. You get the superior feel and handling of cotton with the strength of synthetic thread. Medium or heavy machine thread should be used and matched with the size of the needle.

To simplify your bobbin collection and to avoid frequent change of thread, use large spools of unbleached, natural coloured thread. It goes with just about any colour and saves a lot of time and effort.

Machine sewing is perhaps less of an art than hand seaming but a very pleasurable exercise nonetheless. Each stitch should be perfectly balanced between the upper and lower thread tension as seen in the cross-section drawing.

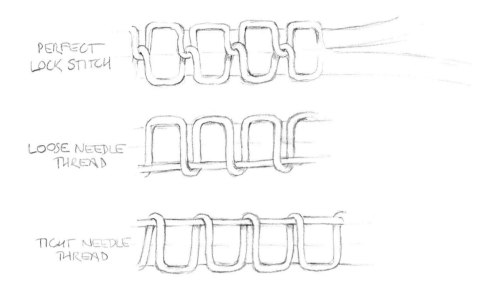

PERFECT
LOCK STITCH

LOOSE NEEDLE
THREAD

TIGHT NEEDLE
THREAD

ADJUSTMENT IS NORMALLY MADE TO THE
NEEDLE THREAD TENSION BUT THAT
PRESUPPOSES THAT THE BOBBIN THREAD
IS AT THE CORRECT, MODERATE SETTING.

Adjustment begins with a basic setting for the bobbin thread, effected with a small screwdriver on the small screw on the bobbin holding down a thread tension plate. There should be just a touch of tension on the bobbin thread, no more. Begin and finish every seam with a couple of back or double stitches to as to secure it against unravelling. With a forward only machine, lift the presser foot and move it back to restitch the first part.

When working with sail cloth and canvas, make sure that the weight of the material is not pulling on the area passing under the presser foot. If it does, lift the work or have someone assist you.

Adjust the tension on the presser foot experimentally until you are familiar with the changes in feeding characteristics that can be effected. Still, you should not rely entirely on the tension between presser foot and feed dog to pull through the material, but be prepared to help it along, especially with heavy cloth on a slippery surface such as yarn-tempered Dacron.

A break occurs in the needle thread if it has been incorrectly threaded. Threading the wrong way is easily done as some machines are threaded from left to right (my Adler, for instance) while others (my Featherweight Singer – American made) will only accept thread in the opposite direction.

The thread may also break if too coarse for the size of needle used. If the machine starts skipping stitches, the likely cause is a bent or incorrectly set needle.

Read, I mean really do, read the instruction book. My 64-page Adler booklet has everything from which way the needle is threaded to crafty little hints about how to re-thread without having to lick and shape the end. You simply cut off the thread on the diagonal with scissors.

3

Canvas

Do not look for canvas at Aswan.

In Egypt, I had kept an eye open for Egyptian cotton, the sailmaking material of my boyhood.

On the Nile waterfront at Aswan, a felucca sailor called Ali, when asked about the supply of cotton sail cloth, gave me a map filled with hieroglyphics.

Upon showing the paper to a man swathed in brown cloth near the Badr Cinema, I was given an escort of small boys. They quickly led the way through back streets to a plain stone dwelling. A fat, noble-looking fellow appeared at the door in a white garment.

He courteously invited me into a central room with a white divan. Here, several members of his family were assembled and he pressed me to sit down and partake of scented tea.

While we sipped out of silver cups, the master of the house perused my map. The case was openly discussed among the family and an increasing number of friends who were arriving to stand at the door.

My host's small daughter was ushered in by older females and offered to translate. Unfortunately, she only knew the word 'hello', and 'do you speak English?'

In the end, we bravely bid goodbye, no one any the wiser, and I bought my cotton in a Cairo supermarket.

You will, I hope, have less difficulty. Cotton canvas has made a comeback against the tide of synthetic weaves and usually weighs 6–12 oz per square yard.

The choice of colours is often limited to natural, white and inky blue, but royal blue, brown and green may also be found.

Very light cotton is sometimes sold under the name of tent cloth and can be a fine choice for sun awnings.

In a blend with synthetics, cotton retains many of its virtues but mixtures are not common in canvas work and the step from pure cotton tends to be to acrylic canvas. Virgin canvas is well served with a mildew proofing administered by the manufacturer but you should always take care to avoid moisture traps and design for free air flow.

The most common width nowadays is just over a metre or 40 in but in work with canvas bags and such there is much to be said for narrower widths as the non-fraying selvedges can be more readily utilised.

Dacron canvas can be cut with a hot-knife – either a professionally made, electric-powered one or an old knife heated on the stove. This seals the fibres and makes a tolerable non-fraying edge; if the canvas is not taut along the edge as is necessary for tabling, it should be turned over at least once.

Lastly, it must be kept in mind that the shrinkage in natural canvas can easily reach eight per cent. In factory-proofed qualities, it may stop at four per cent. Allowance must be made for this when planning and marking up the work. An alternative is to pre-wash the canvas but it will not be as easy to work with in that state, becoming softer and less stable.

Acrylic canvas, available in standard weights of between 8–10 oz as well as a very attractive light weight, is the nearest alternative to cotton in nautical sewing projects. It has the appearance, and resistance to mildew and breakdown from ultra-violet rays, characteristic of cotton. One drawback is that it is quickly damaged by chafing but strategically placed patches can guard against that. It is water resistant but breathes enough to serve in sail and boat covers.

Nylon, also known by trademarks as Oxford (in light weights) and Cordura (in heavy weights), is strong and resistant to abrasion but is weakened by ultra-violet rays. It stretches freely, especially when wet. The surface finish varies but is usually water-resistant while allowing the fabric to breathe.

To handle, and in appearance, nylon is less stable and more glossy than acrylic. Mark up and creasing are more difficult on account of its glossy surface and a resistance to keeping a crease. It sees most use in sail bags.

I'm no great hand at mathematics, but here is a chart which gives a fair idea of how imperial weight for canvas works out against the metric system:

$$6 \, oz = 259 \, g/m^2 \text{ (grams per square metre)}$$
$$7 \, oz = 302 \, g/m^2$$
$$8 \, oz = 345 \, g/m^2$$
$$9 \, oz = 388 \, g/m^2$$
$$10 \, oz = 431 \, g/m^2$$
$$11 \, oz = 474 \, g/m^2$$
$$12 \, oz = 517 \, g/m^2$$

Polyester or Dacron is the first choice for sails proper with surface treatments ranging from none at all to heat-rolling which fuses the fibres together to a smooth, brittle surface. The unfinished cloth is very strong, and resists stretch. Some finishes help guard against ultra-violet breakdown.

'Spun' Dacron is water-resistant and breathes, and there are vinyl-coated, non-breathing but completely waterproof finishes like Weblon. Even when unfinished, polyester does not feel as close to cotton as acrylic.

When cleaning very dirty, heavy canvas of any sort, sand can be sprinkled over it before scrubbing it down with a brush and detergent, removing encrusted dirt. A stiff brush does good work used on its own, too.

After making a few smaller projects, you will have had a chance to work with the range of materials available and take your pick. There is no better material for hand seaming and general handling than cotton, but it is not the best choice for, say, a sprayhood made to close tolerances where it will be loose or tight on the frame depending on if it is fine or wet weather. Also, consistently damp conditions will inevitably produce black mildew spots or even mould.

Canvas Hardware

Tools for canvas work are not a big investment and the dedicated canvas worker or cruising man is bound to profit in the end. You can of course proceed like the Turks and the Egyptians, on sheer ingenuity, but the basic set of die and puncher for No. 1 spur teeth grommets is a boon that I, for one, value highly.

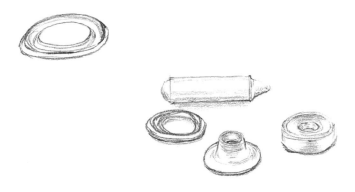

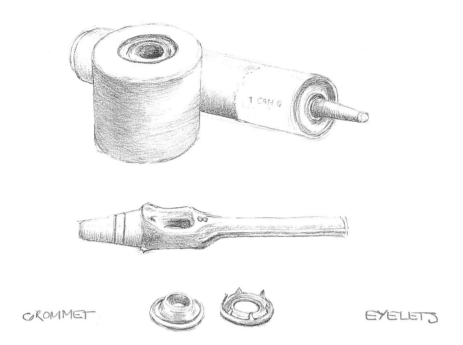

GROMMET   EYELETS

With it, you need a hole punch. To make a strong grommet, clinching well over canvas, the hole should be made one size too small so it needs to be reamed open with a fid to fit the eyelet part. Try to find a Delrin-type cutting board which makes an even better base for this type of work than wood.

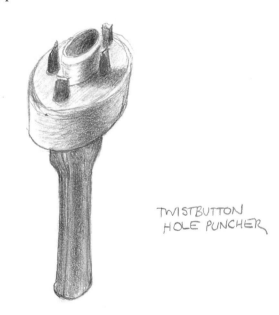

TWISTBUTTON
HOLE PUNCHER

With the eyelet on the die and the punch bearing on the spur toothed ring, apply a compact sledgehammer from above. An ordinary hammer makes indifferent work of it. With a really heavy tool the job is done neatly and without having to strike from different angles.

I would totally forego the alternative of an ordinary eyelet set with cheap gunmetal punch and die and lacking the spur teeth. It works but you need strong faith to think the eyelets will stay in under exceptional pressure.

The grommet eyelet's role is to anchor the luff piston hanks or to edge a sail cover or boat awning. For sail clews, you need a sewn ring, the tooling for which is becoming scarce. If you find a set, along with a good quantity of rings and thimbles, buy it!

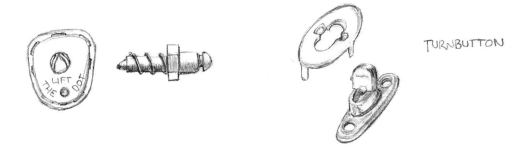

TURNBUTTON

In canvas work, you will also need hardware in the fabric fastener category. The most common type is perhaps the Twist Button which is available with different style base metal to fit either canvas to canvas or canvas to boat. The nickel-plated steel is usually made to last and the attachment is secure and easily opened. A special punch is available to make the canvas hole needed to fit the 'eye' portion. Another type is the Lift-The-Dot style, also well thought out but fiddlier to handle and best applied to limited spreads of canvas.

Canvas Mark-up

The first requirement for marking up canvas prior to cutting to size and sewing is a level floor. These are hard to come by afloat but I have laid out many sails for re-cutting or repair on the dock which, if well chosen, serves just as well on a sunny day.

A particular favourite must be the well-manicured marina or yacht club fore-shore, but the pier in Kaş served well enough too.

For smaller canvas work, any level patch on deck or indoors will usually suffice.

The job calls for care, as any slips are paid for dearly by and by as the work progresses.

The canvas is alike on either side but you should pay attention to the non-fraying selvedges which can be utilised to save the number of tuckovers you need to make to secure the edges.

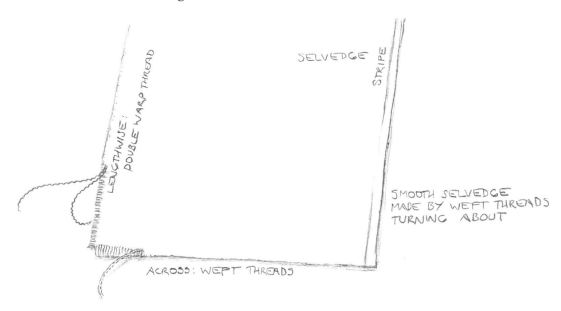

LENGTHWISE: DOUBLE WARP THREAD

SELVEDGE STRIPE

SMOOTH SELVEDGE MADE BY WEFT THREADS TURNING ABOUT

ACROSS: WEFT THREADS

A tape measure marked in metric and imperial measurements is handy. If there is a handle at the end it can be weighed down or fixed with a pricker so that two people need not participate in measuring. A metal tape can even be used to draw guidelines, but wooden battens are usually the best for that.

Draw with chalk or pencil. On white canvas, use an oval carpenter's pencil. Unlike with an ordinary pencil, the point does not break or get stuck. The oval shape should be aligned with the direction of the line drawn.

On blue or other colour canvas, a white wax crayon comes into its own. The most common mark-up is tablings so if you have a batten the width of your usual tabling it will do yeoman service.

Mark up on one side of the canvas, then turn the piece over. With the edge of the canvas turned up, crease along the pencil lines. Use a blunt knife or the back of a clasp knife blade to put in a hard crease.

With your workpiece marked up properly and creased hard, half the job is done.

4
The ditty bag

When I made my first ditty bag at Southwest Harbor in Maine a good few years ago, it was designed to carry large traditional fids and marlinspikes and was 12 in (33 cm) high. There was little use for such windjammer gear on the *Moth* and the big spikes were left at home.

POCKENHOLTZ FID (210 MM)

Gradually, between northern Europe and the Levant, the vacancy was filled by an array of rig adjustment and marine toilet dismantling gear. With spanners collecting at the bottom of the long-necked bag, it was quite a trick to get hold of the right one.

A dozen years after its date of manufacture, the bottom part wore out in Luka Gruz. I cut off the worn part and shortened the bag to 11½ in (29 cm) as I sewed on a new bottom. The refurbished bag was put back on duty as a portable, soft, tool bag – but crowded with hard, angular bedfellows, the hand seaming gear wanted a new bag for its own use.

After making a small bag that one did not have enough room to grope around in comfortably, I settled on one 9½ in (24 cm) high and 16½ in (42 cm) in circumference which has proved handy. A bag that has to go aloft should be an inch less in circumference and half an inch taller.

This is how you can hand sew a small canvas bag to house twine and needles, a hand seaming palm, a lump of beeswax, and a sharp clasp knife. The sharp knife is an elusive thing. A stainless steel blade is corrosion resistant but will not take the keen edge you need. A carbon steel blade makes for a good edge and should be drawn over an oilstone as soon as it gets dull. Polish it if there is any sign of corrosion; oil lightly if the knife is stored.

These are a good start in your inventory but, on emptying the bag for a wash recently, I found the following fellow travellers firmly entrenched:

Swedish fid. This hollow-coned, stainless steel tool deals with wire and rope with equal ease, allowing an opening to pass the cordage in splicing. It's also handy for reaming open a cringle or eyelet hole. The 7 in (18 cm) length is handy for splicing wire strops and mooring line work for boats up to 35–40 feet.

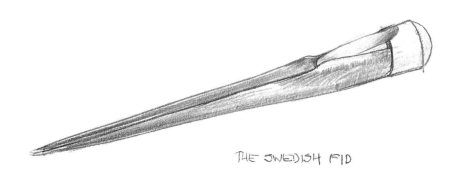

THE SWEDISH FID

Wire cutters. The small spring-loaded variety cut not only wire but any piece of small gauge metal on board. I use them even for snipping off twine.

Tailor's shears. For the genoa work on the dock in Vedbaek I acquired a pair of sturdy centre offset shears nine inches long. Contrary to traditional sailmaking practice, I use them a lot.

Channel-lock pliers. These chrome vanadium pliers are also known as Polygrips and, in Italy, as 'pappagalli'. With a six-inch one you can pull a stuck hand seaming needle through – gently, now!

But on to the bag itself. Look first for stable 12 oz (about 500/g per m²) cotton canvas.

With a carpenter's pencil, measure and draw the plan of the body of the bag on the canvas. The material should be given a 1½ in (3.8 cm) allowance all round and an extra half inch (13 mm) tuck border along the edges and the top – unless the top is a selvedge that does not need a tuck.

Lay the canvas with the pencil mark-up facing down and crease along the pencil lines. The outside half inch creases should be put together as shown in the drawing below to make a total overlap of 1½ in as the first flat seam is put in. Keep the workpiece across your right knee, seaming from right to left with doubled, waxed twine and a No. 15 sail needle.

If you sit low and have a canvas or bench hook attached to your right as shown

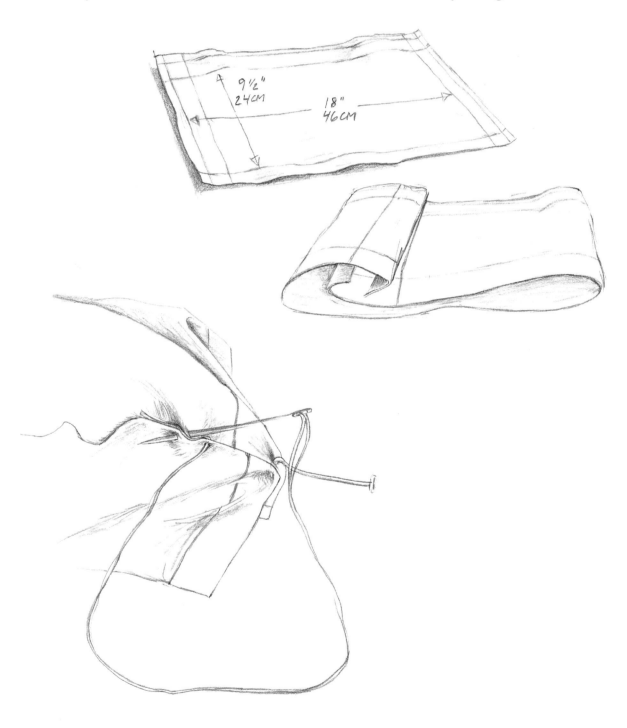

in the last drawing, the work will be more comfortable and the two sides of canvas have a better chance of being matched accurately.

Make three stitches per inch and sew in the end of the twine as you take the first. Finish by taking two back stitches and cutting the twine.

Turn the body of the bag inside out and put in a second seam, a round seam this time. It is taken from left to right, again sewing in the end of the doubled twine with the first few stitches. A canvas hook can again apply tension from the right. The edges of the canvas to be sewn should meet at the pencil mark up lines.

Should you run out of twine at any point, cut the end down to 2 in (5 cm) and thread another fathom on your needle. After twisting and waxing it, twist the doubled end together with the 2 in fag end, tuck the quadrupled twine between the edges of the canvas, and sew over.

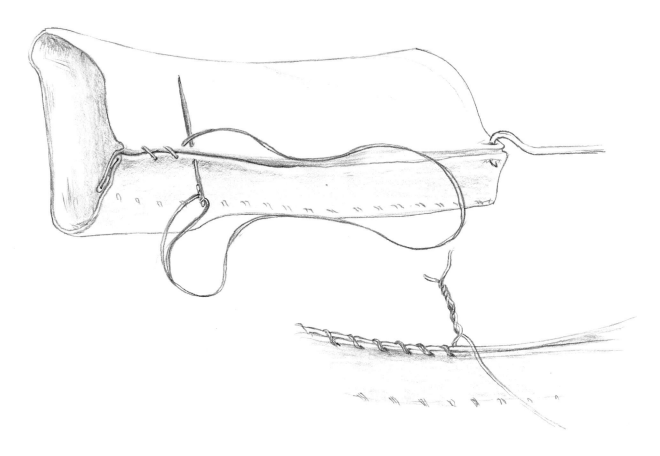

Turn the bag right-side-out (the round seam was on the inside), tuck over and crease the half inch allowance at the top of the bag and then the 1½ in one so the raw edge of the first tuck disappears. The creasing is best done with the back of a knife blade.

If you want a decorative fringe on the bag, cut a broad strip of canvas from along a selvedge on a spare piece and sew it in as a flat seam is taken right around the top of the bag to fix the folded over tabling.

Stand the half-finished bag on its head on another scrap of canvas and pencil a line around the perimeter to mark up the size of the bottom. The canvas should be at least as heavy as the body of the bag, and heavier if you can locate such a piece. An alternative is to double the bottom.

If the mark-up line wavers, find a bowl or tin corresponding to the diameter drawn and use that to help make a proper circle. Draw a line 1½ in outside the first circle and cut the canvas out from that.

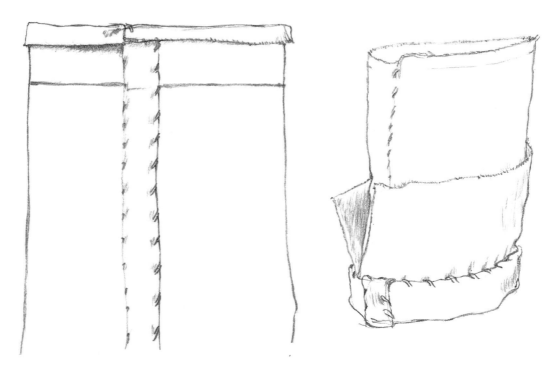

Turn the body of the bag inside out and crease down the one and a half bottom seam allowance. Join the bottom piece to the bag with a round seam along the pencilled in guidelines. Knowing the strain on this seam I make a practice of going round the bottom twice, using the first round of holes to make a formidably strong handmade zig-zag pattern.

The most common way of making eyelets is to put in No.1 brass eyelets with a puncher and die. But as you may not yet have such equipment to hand, why not sew in laid rope grommets? Take a bit of soft three-strand line – small stuff – and cut a length which will go at least three times round the size of the intended hole.

Unlay the strands, take one out and weave it around itself overhand fashion

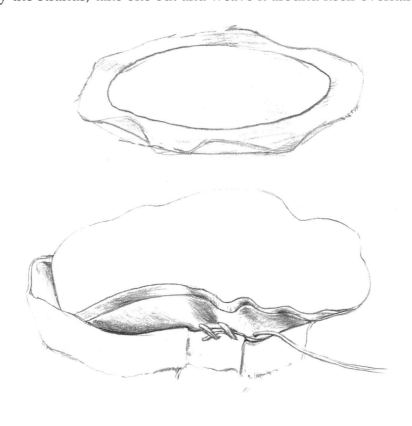

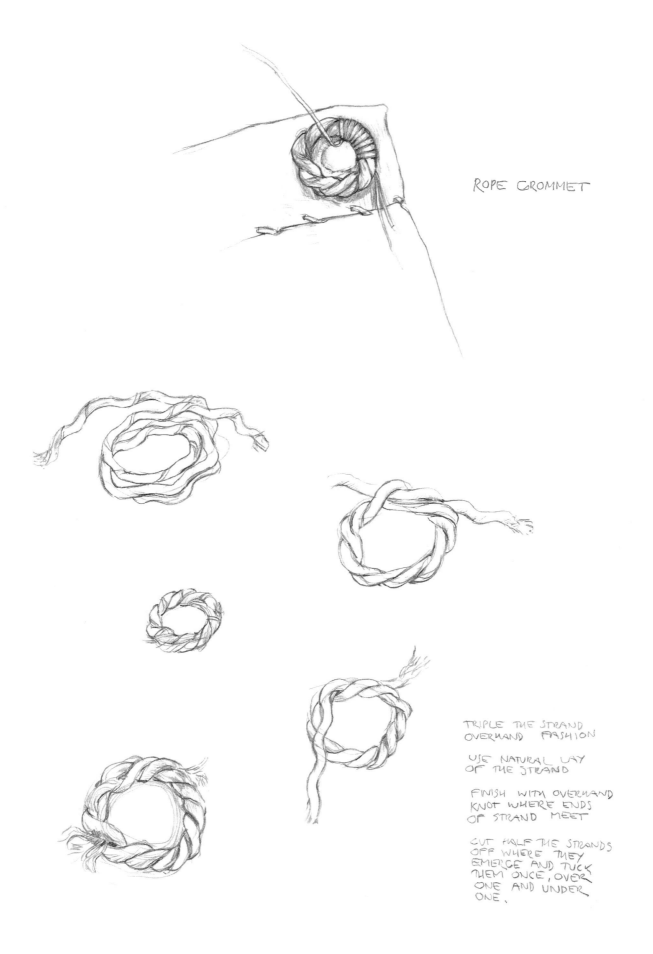

ROPE GROMMET

TRIPLE THE STRAND
OVERHAND FASHION

USE NATURAL LAY
OF THE STRAND

FINISH WITH OVERHAND
KNOT WHERE ENDS
OF STRAND MEET

CUT HALF THE STRANDS
OFF WHERE THEY
EMERGE AND TUCK
THEM ONCE, OVER
ONE AND UNDER
ONE.

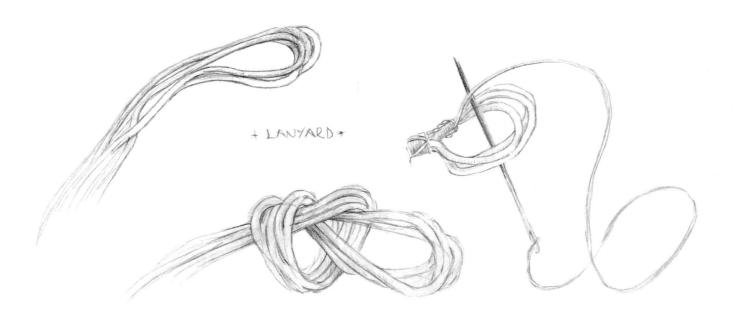

+ LANYARD +

START AS SHOWN

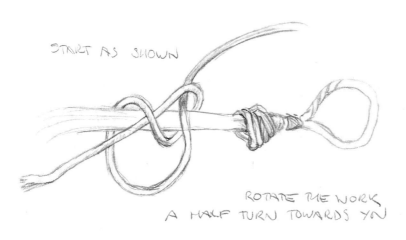

ROTATE THE WORK
A HALF TURN TOWARDS YOU

TUCK LEFT LOOP INTO RIGHT

PASS WORKING END THROUGH
LOOP

ROTATE THE
WORK A HALF
TURN TOWARDS
YOU AND TUCK
THE WORKING END
UP NEXT TO THE
STANDING PART
AND START
DOUBLING UP

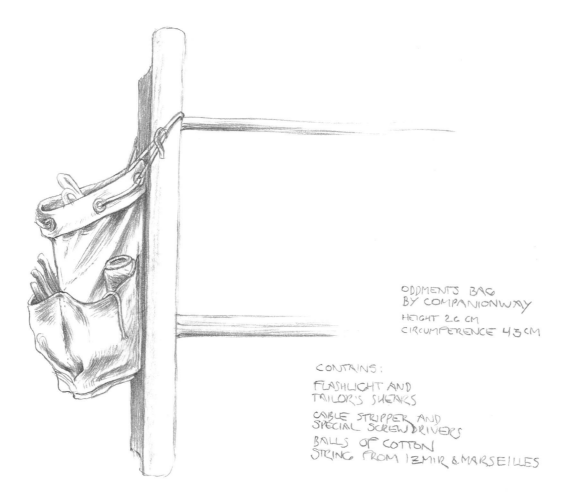

ODDMENTS BAG
BY COMPANIONWAY
HEIGHT 26 CM
CIRCUMFERENCE 45 CM

CONTAINS:
FLASHLIGHT AND
TAILOR'S SHEARS
CABLE STRIPPER AND
SPECIAL SCREWDRIVERS
BALLS OF COTTON
STRING FROM IZMIR & MARSEILLES

until you have a three-strand lay the size of the cringle. Finish with an overhand knot where the ends meet. Cut half the fibres off where the strands emerge and tuck the trimmed ends once before cutting.

Mark up the lanyard holes. In the present example, there are six holes, spaced about 80 mm apart. Cut a hole the size of a penny (or dime) and sew the cringle to the inside of the top of the bag.

The ditty bag lanyard is made either from a doubled, three-strand rope with an eye seized in the middle and the strands unlaid from there, or from three lengths of small stuff with an overhand knot in the middle to make a lanyard eye. Make fast the lanyard with bowlines in the grommets. Seizings are another alternative but make sure the 'legs' are well matched before fixing them.

A Turk's head of three leads and five bights – as simple as they come – will serve to open and close the bag conveniently as it slides up and down the lanyard.

After the initial turns on the Turk's head have been taken and the working end comes alongside the inert end (the 'standing part', in rope-working terms), you just double and then triple the first lead, making tucks to follow it accurately.

Work the leads out to the right amount of tension against the lanyard and cut the ends, not too close.

Let your imagination work in making the trasselling pattern. One word though: it is easier to unravel the cloth if you cut it in inch-wide strips first.

By the end of the *Moth*'s Mediterranean journey, crossing Biscay in October, I got held up by heavy gales in St Peter Port on Guernsey. The boat still lacked a jack of all trades ditty bag permanently fixed by the companionway steps. Finding a scrap of extremely heavy but wonderfully soft Turkish cotton canvas, I made a bag with an extra flap sewn to the outside, as shown, to make small items more readily accessible. The bag has since proved indispensable.

5

Patching

A small tear in a Dacron sail is best patched by machine stitching on another piece of Dacron, similar in weight and finish and with the warp and weft aligned with those of the underlying sail.

   The best patching material to have on board is a few rolls of Dacron tape in 3–4 in widths (8–10 cm). If the patch material is taken from material that does not have the two selvedges (non-fraying borders) of the tape, all four sides have to be tucked under. With tape, tucking the ends is sufficient.

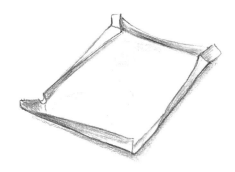

1. CUT A PATCH COVERING A CLEAR 2" · 5CM · OUTSIDE DAMAGE IN THE SAIL

2. DRAW A PENCIL LINE ALL AROUND THE PATCH, ½" · 13MM FROM THE EDGE. CREASE HARD ALONG THE LINE.

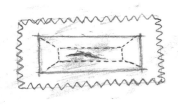

3. WITH THE EDGE TUCKED UNDER, LAY THE PATCH OVER THE RIP. TRACE THE OUTLINE WITH A PENCIL AND KEEP THE PATCH LINED UP AS YOU PUT A ZIG-ZAG STITCH (OR FLAT SEAM, IN HANDSEAMING) ALL ROUND

4. TURN OVER THE SAIL AND DRAW A LINE 1" · 2.5 CM · INSIDE THE STITCH. CUT CLEAR THE DAMAGE AND MAKE MITRE-CUTS TOWARD THE CORNERS OF THE 1" GUIDE LINE; AS PER THE DOTTED LINES.

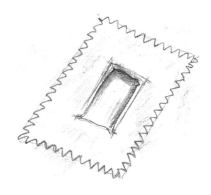

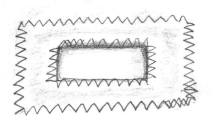

5. FOLD AND CREASE THE FLAPS AND TUCK THEM IN AGAINST THE PATCH.

6. ZIG-ZAG OR FLAT SEAM ALL ROUND TO FINISH.

For those who have a sewing machine on board or the opportunity of taking the sail to a machine ashore, a zig-zag machine stitch should be used.

If you have no access to a sewing machine, thread a fathom of twine, double twist and wax it, and substitute a flat hand seam for the zig-zag. Use waxed machine thread and the smallest sized needle compatible with the weight of your sail.

HAND SEAM PATCHING:

1. CUT A PATCH COVERING A CLEAR 50 MM (2") OUTSIDE DAMAGED SAIL CLOTH

2. FOLD OVER AND CREASE DOWN A 10 MM (1/4") TUCK ALL ROUND.

TURN OVER AND ONTO SAIL DAMAGE. TRACE OUTLINE WITH PENCIL FOR SEAMING.

3. PUT IN A FLAT SEAM ALL ROUND

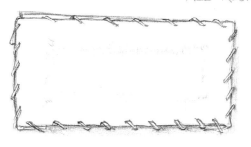

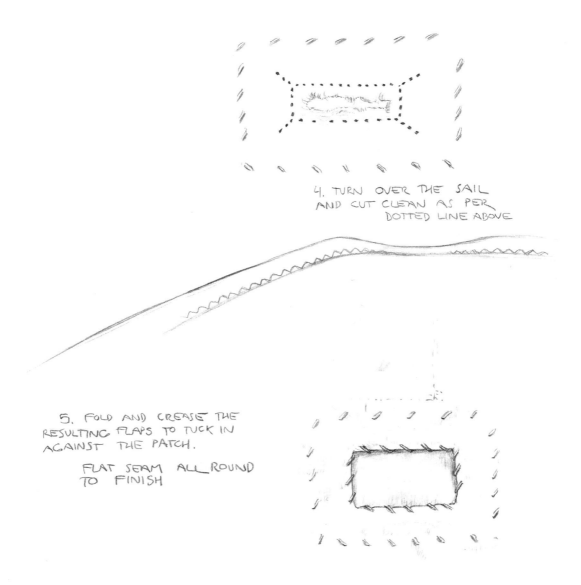

4. TURN OVER THE SAIL AND CUT CLEAN AS PER DOTTED LINE ABOVE

5. FOLD AND CREASE THE RESULTING FLAPS TO TUCK IN AGAINST THE PATCH.

FLAT SEAM ALL ROUND TO FINISH

Large Patching

One blustery day just north of Marstrand, the reefed, 22-year-old mainsail of my vintage wooden '*Andunge*' (Duckling) class yacht, gave way on the leech, just above the shapely but small clew patch.

As the Dacron sailcloth becomes brittle after years of exposure to sun and salt, this is a typical place for a failure in a main. In a headsail, the first tear may come just below the reinforcement patch at the head of the sail.

In such instances, consider if it is worthwhile to make a repair. If the cloth is not totally ripe, when it would tear if pulled moderately, the sail may well stand another few seasons, if used gently.

If the tear is caused by a split pin or other mechanical fault, but the sail itself is in good shape, a repair is certainly worthwhile.

When cloth fatigue is to blame, major distortion occurs in the cloth around the tear. It is therefore often difficult to match up the torn cloth. Nonetheless, with the sail spread evenly on a flat floor, try to tape together the tear as neatly as possible, as shown opposite.

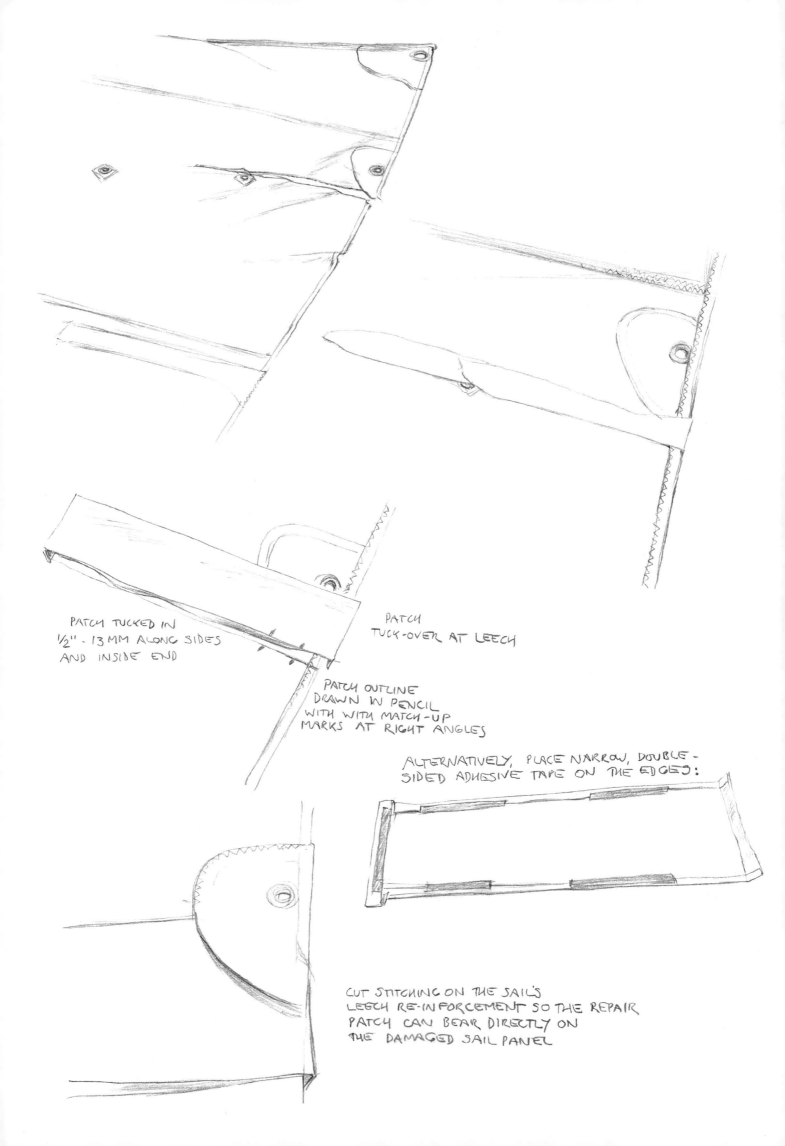

PATCH TUCKED IN
1/2" - 13 MM ALONG SIDES
AND INSIDE END

PATCH
TUCK-OVER AT LEECH

PATCH OUTLINE
DRAWN IN PENCIL
WITH WITH MATCH-UP
MARKS AT RIGHT ANGLES

ALTERNATIVELY, PLACE NARROW, DOUBLE-
SIDED ADHESIVE TAPE ON THE EDGES:

CUT STITCHING ON THE SAIL'S
LEECH RE-INFORCEMENT SO THE REPAIR
PATCH CAN BEAR DIRECTLY ON
THE DAMAGED SAIL PANEL

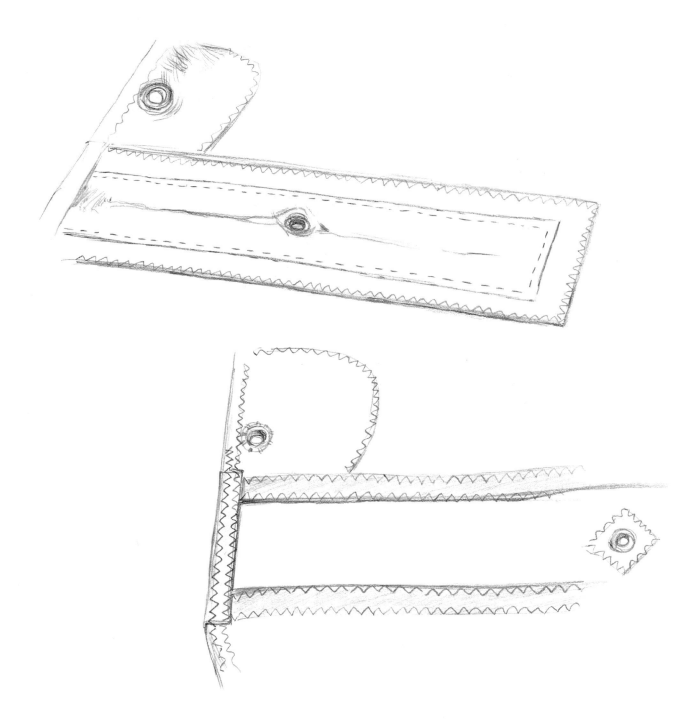

Cut to size a patch which resembles the sailcloth in weight and character and covers the area distorted by the tear. Tuck down and crease the edges of the patch with the back of a clasp knife blade and line it up with the panel in the sail.

To keep the patch in position you can use double-sided sailmaker's tape; but another way is to make an outline of the patch with a carpenter's pencil.

Sew down the outer edge of the patch and turn the sail over.

On the reverse side of the sail, as shown in the last two drawings, first draw a 1½ in (2½ cm) line inside the outside edge of the patch. Draw another half-inch (13 mm) line inside the last guideline, cut out the damaged part of the sail (along the dotted line shown) and tuck under the half-inch wide allowance before putting in the last zig-zag seam all around. Sew on corner patches and replace fittings like the reef eyelet shown.

Rough Patching

In a boat tarpaulin or cover that is rapidly deteriorating, satisfactory repairs can be achieved by using backing pieces, preferably of a similar weight to that of the cover itself.

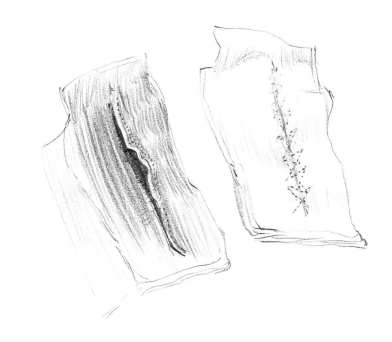

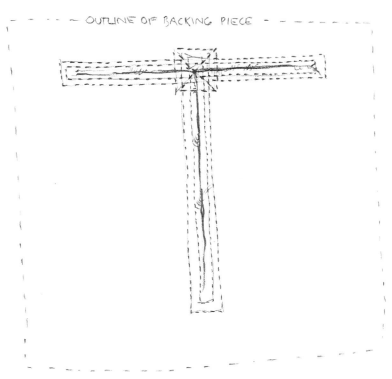

With the backing piece sewn evenly along the edges on the reverse of the damaged area, run a zig-zag freely over the torn edges. A straight seam can also be improvised into a zig-zag pattern if the presser foot is let up.

Another alternative is to isolate the tear with double rows of straight stitching as in the drawing of a T-shaped tear.

6

The small heavy-duty bag

The ditty bag and the sea bag fulfil many needs but the small utility bag also does a good job in sheltering your spare shackles, coinage or cycle repair kit. The minimum height for easy sewing in heavy canvas is 6 in (15 cm) with a circumference of 11 in (28 cm). To draw up the canvas needed, add a 2 in (2.5 cm) allowance at the bottom, a 1½ in (3.8 cm) tabling with a half-inch allowance at the top, and 1½ in sewing allowance at either end where the bag will be sewn together with a double turnover seam.

After marking up the canvas and cutting it to size outside the allowances, turn it over and insert a hard crease along the half-inch tabling allowance that will meet the 1 in allowance to form the body of the bag. Also crease over the tabling mark-up lines.

Make a cylinder of the canvas with the mark-up on the inside and put in a straight seam after doubling the canvas so the half-inch sewing allowance crease is on top of the 1 in allowance mark-up. Use the crease as a guide to sew along. The tuck will also help in preparation for the next seam which is taken after the 1 in allowance has been folded around the half-inch allowance and the tripled cloth laid against the side of the bag.

The second seam is taken from the unmarked side of the bag, at the outer edge of the tripled canvas lying against the bag side. The distance between the first and second seam will be around half an inch. When sewing it will be necessary to crumple up the cylinder of the bag so that the seams come at least halfway into it. When the going gets difficult, just take the work out of the machine and start at the opposite end of the cylinder – from which you should be able to meet the stitches first taken and complete the joining of the body of the bag. Flatten the bag and make hard creases or pencil marks on the tabling at the outside edges. On either side of the marks low in the tabling, put in small eyelets. Those that come in a kit with special pliers for clinching – of a type once used for making shoelace holes – will answer the present need. Regular spur teeth grommets up to size 1 can also be used, but then it is best to put in a single grommet on either side of the bag, right on the mark. Either way, the 'good', brassy side should face the marked-up side of the bag.

The low placement in the tabling allows a seam to be taken at the halfway line, to allow for easier bunching of the material when the two lanyard ends are put in, as shown. Each makes a turn around the bag and comes out through its own two eyelets (or one grommet, if that is chosen).

When the distance line dividing the tabling has been sewn, taking care not to catch the lanyards, the cords and the half-inch tabling tuck are sewn in along the bottom of the 1½ in wide tabling proper.

Stand the bag on its head on another piece of canvas, at least as heavy as the one used for the body of the bag. Draw a pencil line around the bag with a 1 in wide allowance all around. Cut around the outer line and crease along the inside line. Turn the body of the bag inside out and crease out the half-inch allowance along the bottom. Put in a round seam by hand seaming all around, left to right, sewing in the fag end.

It may seem out of place to end a machine sewing project with hand seaming and I admit that the job can be finished with a single straight machine seam, especially if a single-sided presser foot is used. But what the machine cannot do is to have a sense of the need to match the bottom with the bag. However carefully one measures, one tends to allow for too large a bottom which means that the

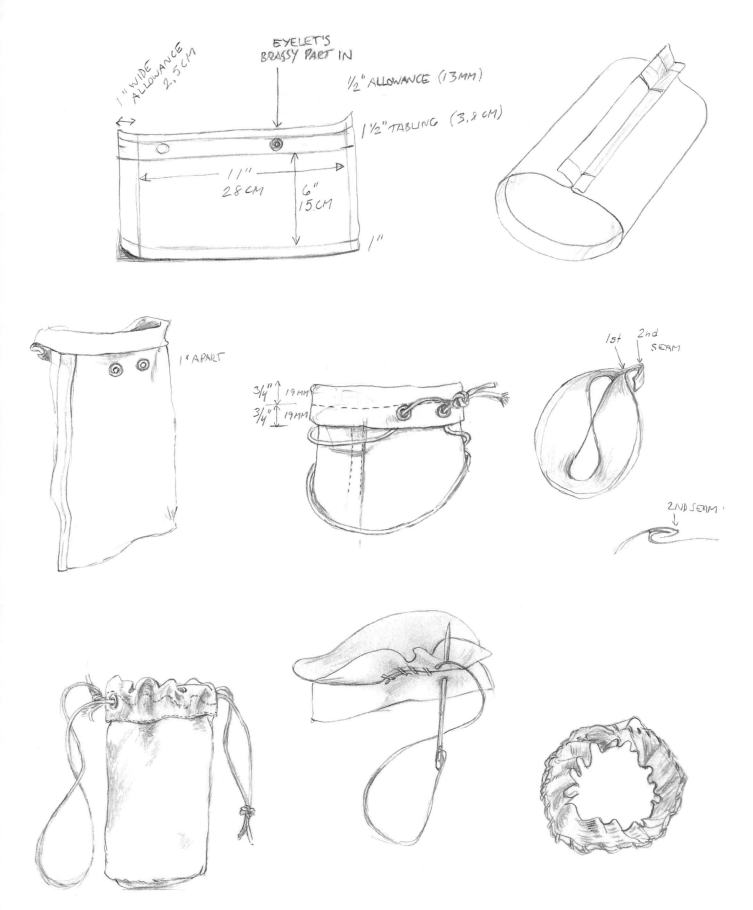

mark-up line on the bottom has to be abandoned for a short cut towards the end of the work. Hand seaming, that is an easy thing to do. Besides, a round seam is a lot stronger than a single straight one.

Turn the work right side out and you can start putting in whatever small things most urgently need a home.

7

The drawstring bag

The simplest bag of all is the drawstring one made in light canvas or calico from a doubled piece.

The *Moth* has two, one for odd bits of canvas and webbing, one for clothes pegs.

Use any spare cloth, 140 in × 17 in (102 cm × 43 cm) will serve nicely, for an oddments bag. Mark up as shown with a 1½ in wide strip bordered on the outside by a further 1½ in width for tucking. Turn the piece upside down. Put a crease along the long sides of the canvas, in the two pencil lines. Tuck the narrow allowance under the wide one and sew down along the doubled edge with a straight seam.

Crease down the two pencil lines at the short end and fold in over the innermost one. Sew down the tabling halfway down, using a faint guideline if necessary. Tuck in two pieces of string as shown on the right and sew down the tabling with the half-inch border tucked under. Make sure the string is contained inside the seam without being nipped by it.

An alternative is to pass a blunted, threaded sail needle (bodkin, size ten or so) through after the sewing is done. Seamstresses pass a safety pin through after hooking a string to it.

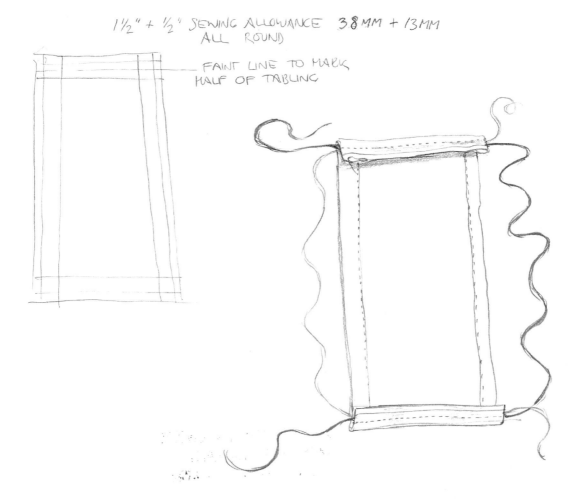

1½" + ½" SEWING ALLOWANCE 38MM + 13MM
ALL ROUND)

FAINT LINE TO MARK
HALF OF TABLING

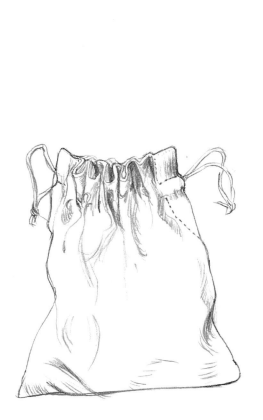
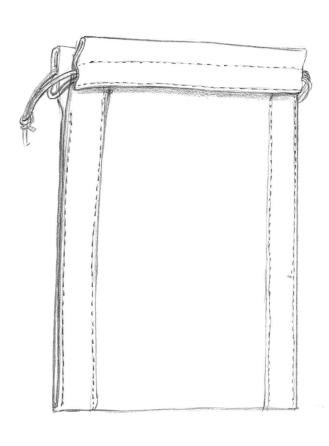

Double up the bag with the mark-up side on the outside and sew from the bottom fold to the tabling on either side. Tie together the string ends with overhand knots.

If you want a flat bottom, turn the bag inside out and sew in the bottom corners as described in the drawing of Turkish style boat cushions on page 82.

8

Toilet kit bag

See if the dimensions of this small zipper bag are sufficient for your toothbrush, shaver and Bay Rum bottle – or Rive Gauche and moisturising lotion as the case may be – by making a 1:1 paper model.

Lay down the dimensions on sturdy 10 oz cotton canvas with a carpenter's pencil. If you think the canvas is too heavy for such a small bag I would point out that it is precisely in a small bag that the shape and poise is most enhanced by a heavy grade.

Three pieces are needed, two for the sides and one for the bottom and ends.

When cutting the side pieces to size they can be checked for symmetry by folding down the centre as shown by the dotted line in the drawing, and against one another by simply laying one on top of the other.

When satisfied that all is fair, join one side of the bag to the bottom by matching up the edges as shown on page 47 and putting a tabling strip on by means of a straight machine stitch.

Cotton tabling strips are readily available in half-inch (13 mm) widths (folds not counted) but if you are far from civilisation you can cut your own. The trick is to cut these strips out along the diagonal of the cloth. That way, they stretch neatly around corners.

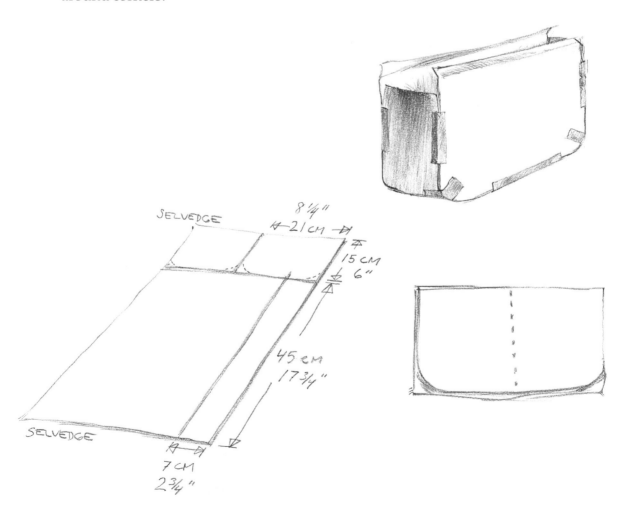

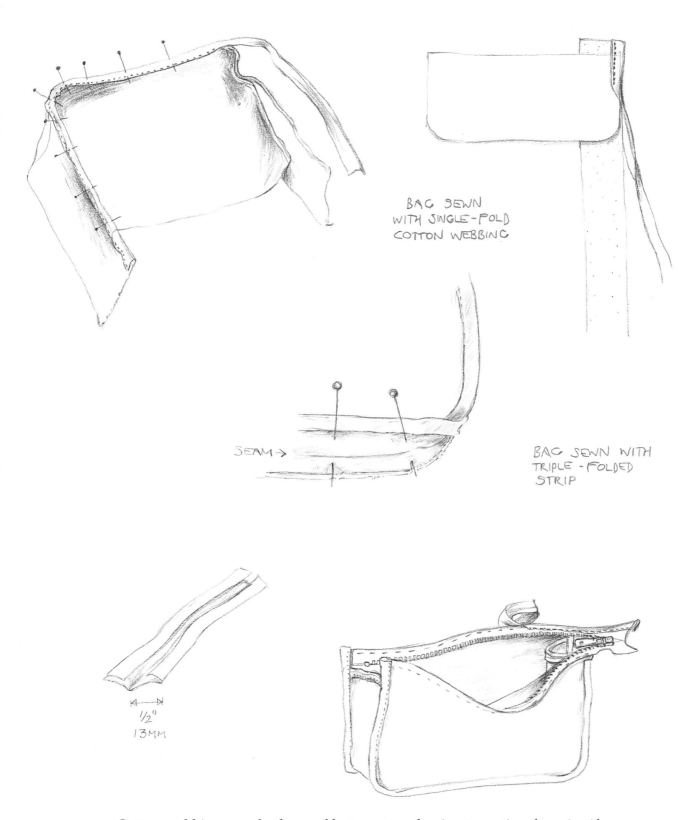

BAG SEWN
WITH SINGLE-FOLD
COTTON WEBBING

SEAM →

BAG SEWN WITH
TRIPLE-FOLDED
STRIP

½"
13MM

Cotton webbing can also be used but count on having to put in a few pins if you hope to catch all four layers in one seam (see the two top drawings).

Handiest by far is the prefabricated pre-folded strip, sticking some pins in as in the detail drawing, the edge of the strip matching to the edges of the canvas, and sewing along the fold. When a straight seam has been taken all around, the pins are taken out and the tabling strip wrapped right around the raw edges and sewed down from the other side. Sew on the second side of the bag the same way.

To close the bag, you will need a non-corroding zipper which should be an inch or two longer than the top of the bag. The zipper is sewn in against the top edges of the sides of the bag and the resulting raw edge is again covered with a tabling strip. Note that the zipper extends over the end of the bag at one end only. Placed thus, it gives you something to hold on to when closing it, especially in overload conditions.

9

The tote bag

A top-opening carryall in light canvas is always useful. For easy work on the sewing machine, pick a canvas weighing 7 oz per yd^2 (300 g per m^2). A 10 oz bag will be more stable, but more difficult to sew.

The traditional colour is bleached or unbleached white but a more cheerful idea is to have the body of the bag in one colour, such as royal blue, and the end pieces, carrying handles and zipper in another, such as contrasting white.

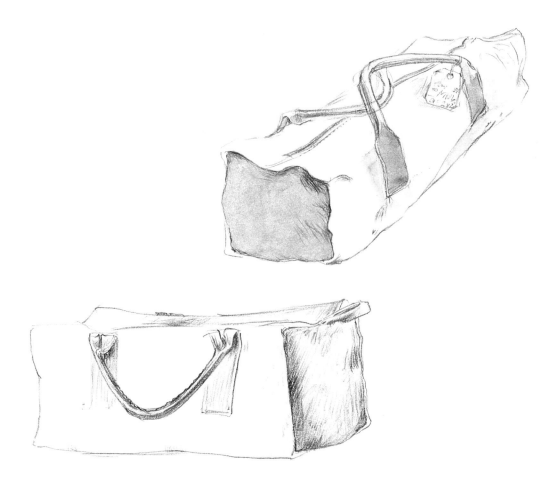

Cut the three pieces of canvas needed to size as shown opposite. Draw a pencil line 1 in in from the long sides of the larger, body piece. This marks the allowance for sewing it together with the two end pieces. On these, there should be a corresponding mark-up half an inch from the edge, drawn all around. Put a hard crease along the pencil lines on the smaller pieces.

Mark up the halfway mark on the long sides of the big piece and on the short sides on the small ones. Match up the markings as shown, with the 1 in sewing allowance lines placed right below the half-inch allowance lines. With a straight stitch, sew together the outside end of one end piece with the body, along the mark-up, but without going beyond the 'margin' at either end.

To ensure the two pieces being sewn together in alignment, with the bag body overlapping the end piece by a half-inch, pins can be used to good effect, as shown

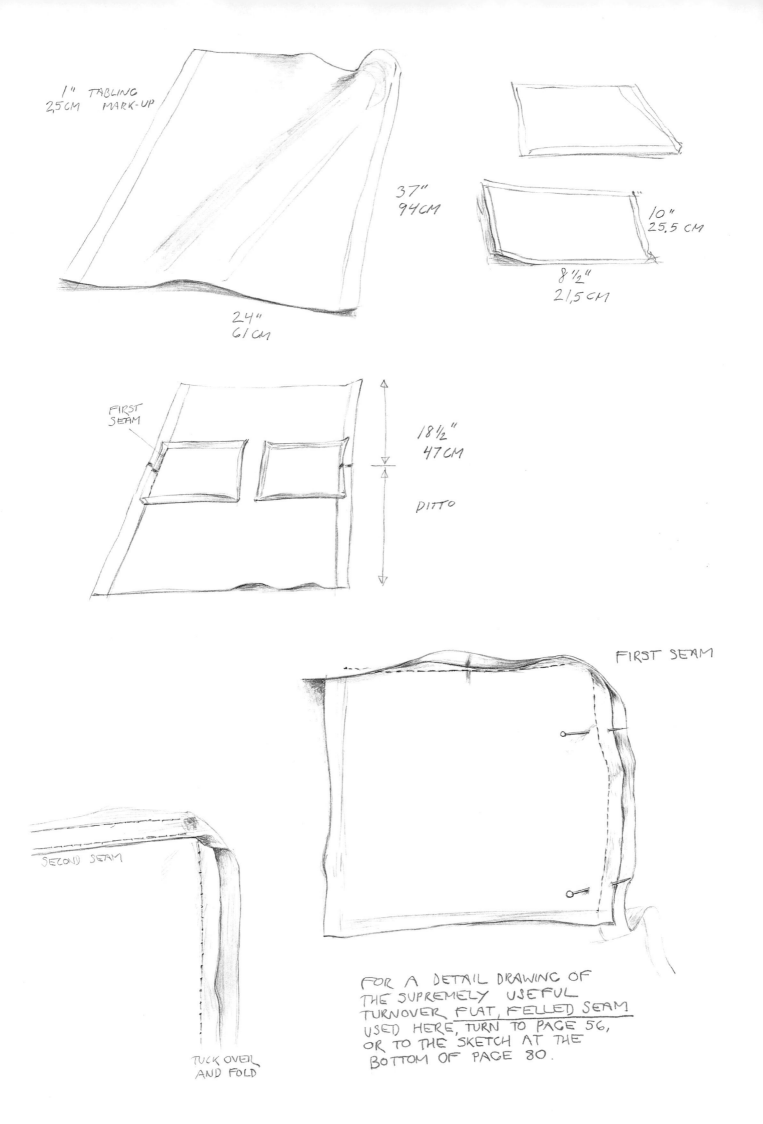

1" TABLING
2,5CM MARK-UP

37"
94CM

10"
25,5 CM

8½"
21,5 CM

24"
61 CM

FIRST
SEAM

18½"
47CM

DITTO

FIRST SEAM

SECOND SEAM

TUCK OVER
AND FOLD

FOR A DETAIL DRAWING OF
THE SUPREMELY USEFUL
TURNOVER FLAT, FELLED SEAM
USED HERE, TURN TO PAGE 56,
OR TO THE SKETCH AT THE
BOTTOM OF PAGE 80.

opposite. Sew up the sides as well and up to the top opening, leaving a 2 in gap at the centre to allow for fitting the zipper. Before taking another seam right round, tuck the overlap in over the edge of the end piece and fold this tripled canvas once more along the first line of stitches, to lie flat against the end piece to which it is now sewn.

Take another double stitch to join the other end piece to the bag. Mark up the body piece where the two ends come together at the top centreline of the bag and crease hard along the centreline. Make another half-inch tuck and hard crease at the edge of the canvas and sew in this double tuck to avoid fraying.

The sewing so far has taken place on the inside of the bag but it can now be turned right side out. Make hard creases between the top corners of the bag and make a mark 5 in from each end. From this, draw a straight line 4 in down the side of the bag.

Make up handles from cotton webbing which should be at least 1 in wide and

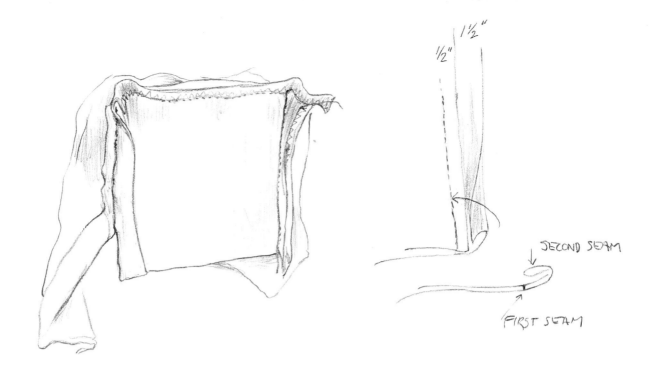

SECOND SEAM

FIRST SEAM

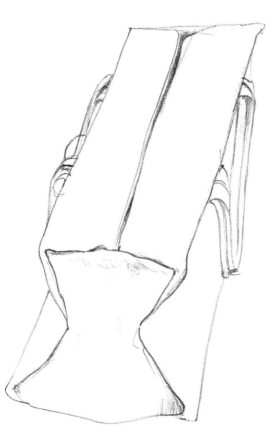

one-eighth of an inch thick. Two lengths, each 26 in long, are needed. Tuck the ends under half an inch before sewing them to the sides of the bag.

Cut a 25 inch length of plastic zipper or buy one of about the length. Sew it to the bag with a straight seam, using a single presser foot attachment if necessary. It is convenient to have the zip project out from the bag a few inches at the closed end to give you something to hold on to when the bag is full and you have to pull hard at the zipper.

To maintain the shape of the bag when full, it helps to insert a heavy piece of cardboard to cover the bottom.

If you choose heavy, 12 oz canvas for your tote bag, it may be difficult to use a fully fledged turnover seam at the ends. The material is unwieldy and the multiple layers may not fit under the presser foot of your sewing machine.

The alternative is to join the canvas at the end with a straight seam with the bag inside out, with a 1½ in and half-inch (3.8 cm and 13 mm) allowance projecting as shown at the top of the page.

WEBBING FOR HANDLES

5" x 28½"

12 CM WIDE
x 72.5 CM

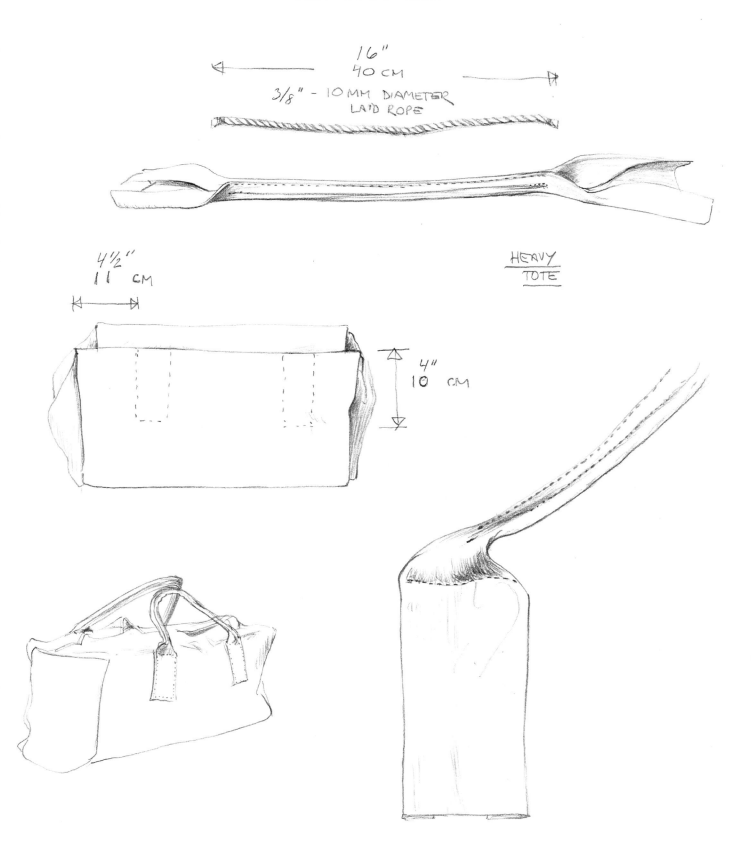

The longer projection is then tucked over the shorter and a zig-zag seam put in to secure the joint and guard against fraying.

The handles can also be strengthened if rope is sewn into a piece of webbing as shown in the drawing. To press the rope well into the sleeve with the second seam, a single presser foot should be used.

In other respects, proceed as with the lighter tote.

10

The seagoing bag

This is for rough usage, with boot, bottom, grommet and end reinforcements. Accordingly, choose sturdy canvas in the 12 oz range.

Lay it down on a level floor and mark up the outline measurements (30 in × 36½ in – 76 cm × 93 cm). Also mark up and cut to size the bottom reinforcement piece and the boot strip and arrange them on the large piece as shown in the drawing. Crease and tuck under a half inch (13 mm) along the near side of the boot reinforcement strip.

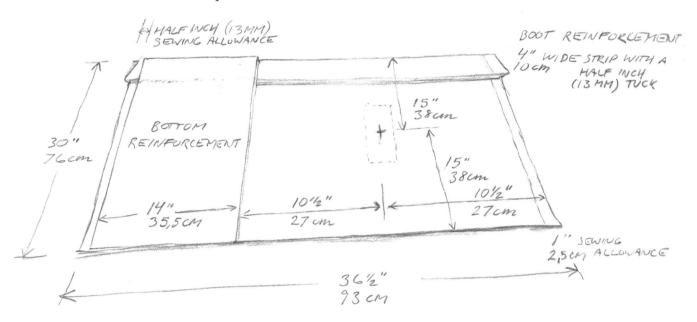

Draw a pencil line along the doubled edge for guidance and sew to the large canvas piece with a single straight seam close to the doubled edge.

Next, crease and tuck under a half-inch wide strip on either side of the bottom reinforcement strip. Place it a half inch from the left side edge of the large piece as shown, edges tucked under, and draw pencil lines to help as it is sewed down with a straight seam close to the doubled edges. Leave the short sides at top and bottom alone.

Cut out and crease a 10 × 3½ in (25 cm × 9 cm) piece of canvas for the handle reinforcement patch. The crease all around should be half an inch wide. On the side, hand sew a short length of rope into a piece of heavy-duty webbing to make a handle. Tuck the ends of the webbing under the short ends of the patch and join them with a straight seam.

On the part of the large canvas not covered by the bottom reinforcement, draw diagonal lines from the corners or measure to find the centre point. Lay the handle reinforcement patch so it centres nicely and sew down with a seam all around.

Turn over the work and fold the left side over to the right so the marked-up half-inch edge lies over the marked up one-inch line. Make a straight seam along this line – along the edge of the bottom reinforcement. Crease the half-inch allowance hard to the left, tuck the 1 in allowance over it, and fold down the tripled cloth to the left. Sew it to the doubled bottom canvas with a straight seam

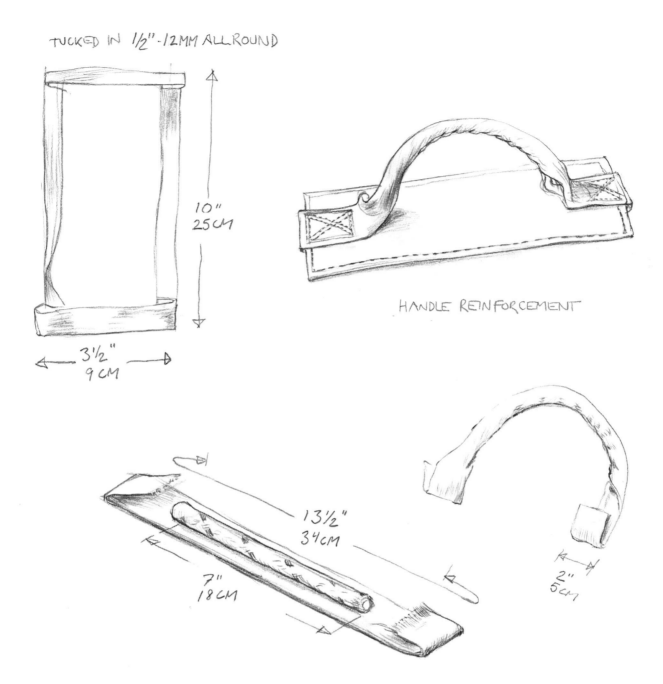

TUCKED IN 1/2".12MM ALL ROUND

10"
25CM

3½"
9CM

HANDLE REINFORCEMENT

13½"
34CM

7"
18CM

2"
5CM

near the edge, flattening the canvas and sewing into the cylinder formed by the large body piece. Sew as far into the canvas cylinder as you easily can – at least halfway – then start again from the other end.

Take care not to catch the underlying cloth to form a figure-of-eight bag.

Turn the cylinder inside out and mark up 1 in (25 mm) wide border at the boot reinforcement end. Crease along the pencil line and turn out. Place the end of the cylinder on a piece of extra heavy or doubled spare canvas and draw a pencil line that follows the bottom outline. Draw another line half an inch outside the first line. Check that you have a pretty even circle before cutting the end piece to size along the outside pencil line. Crease hard along the inner pencil line and match up with the creased edge on the bag.

This is a machine sewing project but I recommend putting the end pieces on by hand seaming. If the circles do not quite match up – and they seldom do – this way of working allows for last minute adjustments.

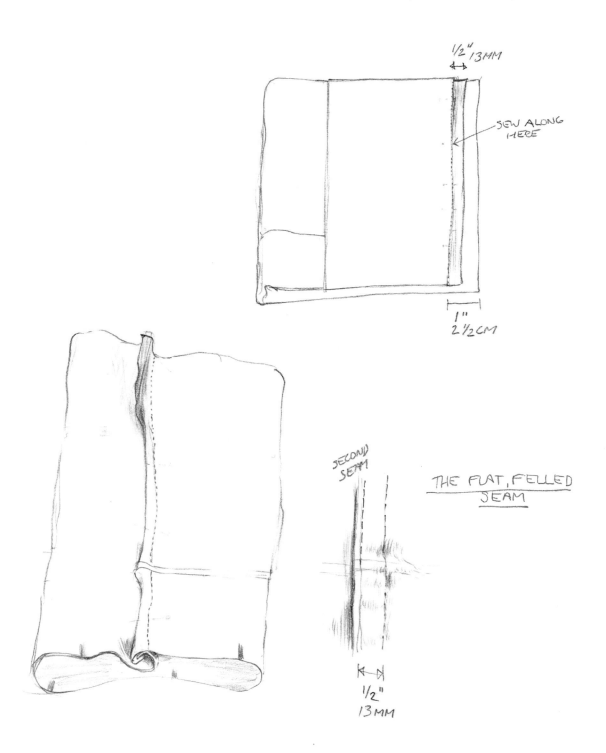

½" 13MM

SEW ALONG HERE

1" 2½CM

SECOND SEAM

THE FLAT, FELLED SEAM

½" 13MM

Thread, double and twist a fathom of waxed twine and, tucking back both the doubled edge of the end piece and the bag, pass a round seam – through, back over and in again – from left to right. Work your way around the circle and take a second turn around in the already made stitches if the first turn does not look strong enough.

Should you not have a palm-and-needle handy, make a straight machine stitch right around after matching up the end piece as shown in the drawing.

For the final touch, prepare a strip of canvas with the same circumference as the open end of the bag. Allow a couple of extra inches and sew the two ends of the

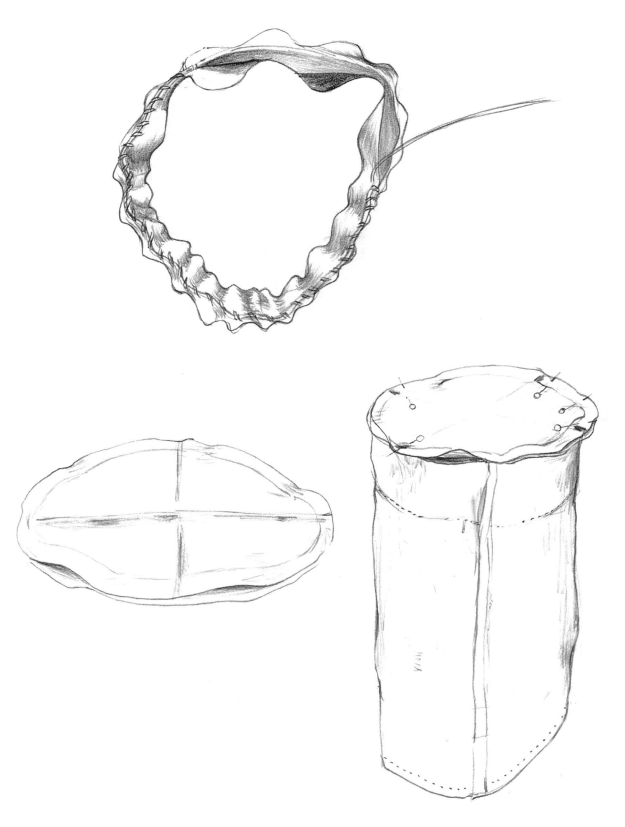

strip together after matching it against the bag mouth. Mark up and crease down a half-inch tuck in this collar, as shown.

With the bag right-side-out, fit this collar over the open end, tucked end foremost. Pull it far enough onto the bag to make the right edge of the strip match up with the right edge of the bag.

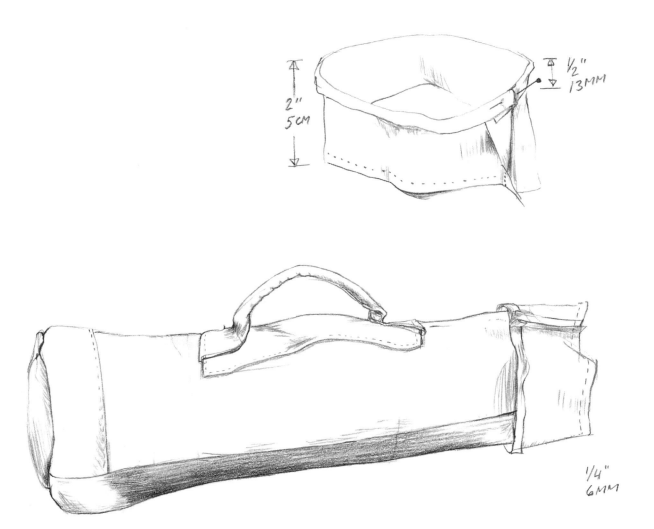

Make a straight seam along the double edge, a quarter-inch (6 mm) from it.

Turn the bag inside out and fold the collar back so the tuck lies neatly under as seen in the drawing. If a canvas flap protecting the content of the bag appeals to you, tuck one in under the edge of the tabling before taking the final seam. To make a flap, cut out two pieces that roughly conform with the circumference of the bag and take a straight seam just inside the doubled edges, stopping short before the circle is complete. Pull the pieces inside out through the remaining hole and fit under the tabling of the bag at that same point.

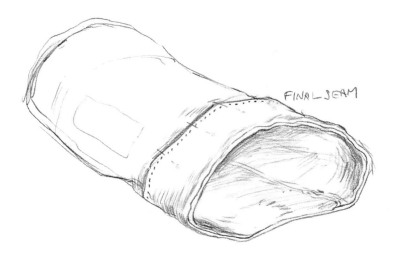

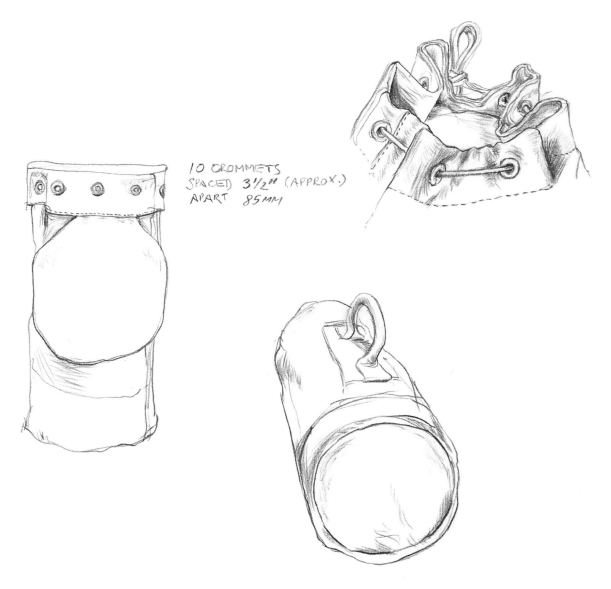

10 GROMMETS
SPACED 3½" (APPROX.)
APART 85MM

    With the bag still inside out, mark up the position of ten grommets along the doubled, open end. Cut the holes and bang them in from the reverse side, to put the brassy grommets out on the front.

    Turn the bag right-side-out and inspect your work.

11

The canvas bucket

On Anti-Paxos I met a New Yorker hailing from Bavaria. He was called Georg and made a living buying boats in one place and selling them in another. He had bought a 42-footer from the yard in Taiwan and shipped it to the Chesapeake where he sold it. With part of the profit, he had bought a Franz Maas-built Standfast on the French Riviera, ten years old but in impeccable condition, with which he was now cruising until a cheap freight was on offer to the United States.

The appearance of the Standfast was further improved by a sturdy canvas bucket with a wooden bottom. It was hanging from one of the winches at the foot of the mast.

Had it come with the boat? No, he had taken it from another boat he had owned briefly.

'It lends it a bit of class,' he said.

I thought the *Moth* could do with some too, and set to work.

A canvas bucket can be made by hand seaming, in much the same way as a ditty bag is hand sewn. A sewing machine makes a little shorter work of it.

The Standfast's bag dimensions of 28 in (71 cm) circumference and 12 in (30 cm) height looked fine so I cut up 12 oz canvas with a 2½ in tabling allowance along the selvedge, another at the joining ends (a half and one inch respectively), with provision for a double tuck at the foot end, as shown in the drawing.

I also secured some half-inch diameter polypropylene cordage to sew in along the rim of the bag.

CIRCUMFERENCE
28"
71 CM

12" HIGH
30 CM

3/4" THICK WOODEN
2 CM BOTTOM

BRONZE OR
COPPER TACKS
SPACED 1½" APART
3.5 CM

CANVAS BUCKET

THE CANVAS BUCKET

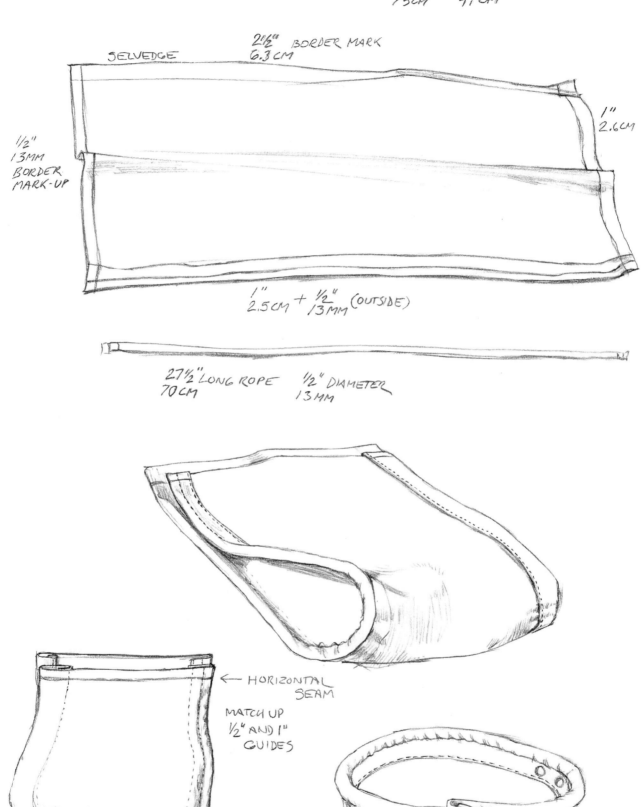

CUT A 29½" × 16" PIECE
75CM   41CM

SELVEDGE

2½" BORDER MARK
6.3 CM

1"
2.6CM

½"
13MM
BORDER
MARK-UP

1"
2.5CM + ½" (OUTSIDE)
13MM

27½" LONG ROPE   ½" DIAMETER
70CM   13MM

← HORIZONTAL
    SEAM

MATCH UP
½" AND 1"
GUIDES

Furthermore, with the workpiece neatly marked with a carpenter's pencil, you have to turn the canvas over and crease over the upper single tuck tabling and the lower double tuck tabling.

With the rope aligned with the upper tuck, sew it in with a straight seam near the selvedge and another hard against the rope, using a single presser foot.

Sew in the lower double tuck with a straight stitch just inside the crease. All three seams are shown in the larger drawing of the folded workpiece.

As the rope is shorter than the workpiece, it stops short of the half and one inch mark-up at the short ends of the canvas.

As shown in the smaller drawing of the folded workpiece, the short ends are matched up so the lower cloth comes a half an inch short of the edge of the underlying one. Make sure you have the rope to the right and take a straight seam as directed by the arrow.

Next, you fold the inch-wide allowance around the half-inch one and, laying them against the canvas body of the bag, take another straight stitch near the folded edge. Sewing the bag cylinder is, you will perceive, another good use for the flat felled seam.

In making attachments for the bucket lanyard, two single eyes need be of greater dimension than two pairs, so, in order to make use of the No.1 Spur Teeth Grommet set most often carried, I opted for two pairs struck into the upper bucket tabling, just bearing against the sewn-in rope. Lacking a grommet set, you can sew in rope grommets made from a tripled single rope strand.

To lay a cringle, the grommets should be close together. The cringle is made with a single strand taken from a metre or 40 in of suitable spare cordage.

Lay as shown in the drawings, starting by winding the ends of the strand back

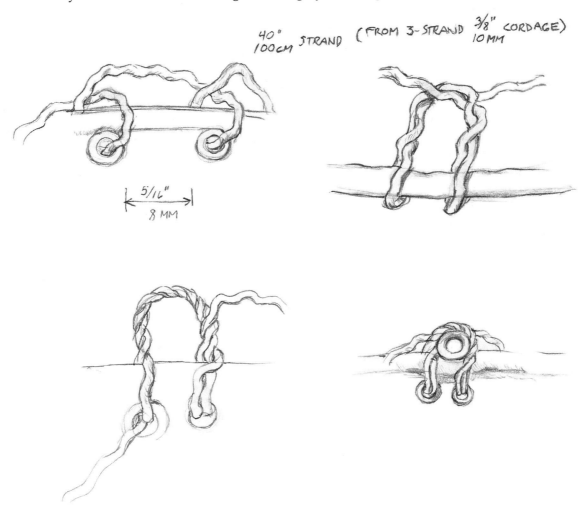

40"
100CM STRAND (FROM 3-STRAND ⅜" CORDAGE)
10 MM

|← 5/16" →|
8 MM

on itself (first drawing); meeting at the top (second drawing); continuing past one another; down through the grommet holes (third drawing); and back up around itself once more until meeting for the last time.

The ends are then tucked over and under a few times before cutting.

If you would like thimbles in the cringles, make the cringles a bit smaller than the size of the thimbles. Ream open the hole with a fid and quickly insert the thimble which will fit more snugly the greater the skill of the hand inserting it.

Thinking thimbles superfluous, I clapped a racking seizing around the middle of the cringles to make them tidy and spliced in a lanyard.

Made from another 40 in of laid rope, this should be unwound up to a length of 4 in (10 cm) at each end to make an eye splice with the ends pulled through the cringles.

To make an eye splice in three strand cordage, tuck in the middle strand first, under one strand, against the lay of the rope.

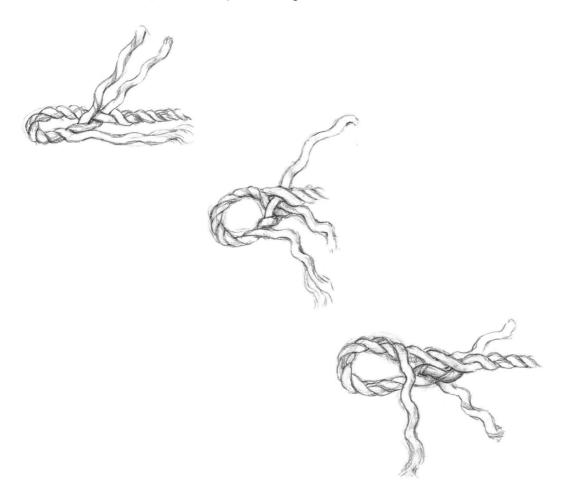

The next tuck is the strand nearest to the eye in the rope. Lastly, tuck in the remaining strand.

Tuck in all three a second and third time, over one and under one, against the lay. Draw home and cut the ends with an allowance of at least half an inch (13 mm).

With the lanyard spliced in, double it up so you have the balance point at the loop end. Put a seizing in to make an eye into which a rope can be fastened for throwing the bucket over the side of the boat to catch water.

Before attempting this, you will need to locate a three-quarter inch (2 cm) or so thick piece of softwood like elm on which you can draw the outline of the bottom

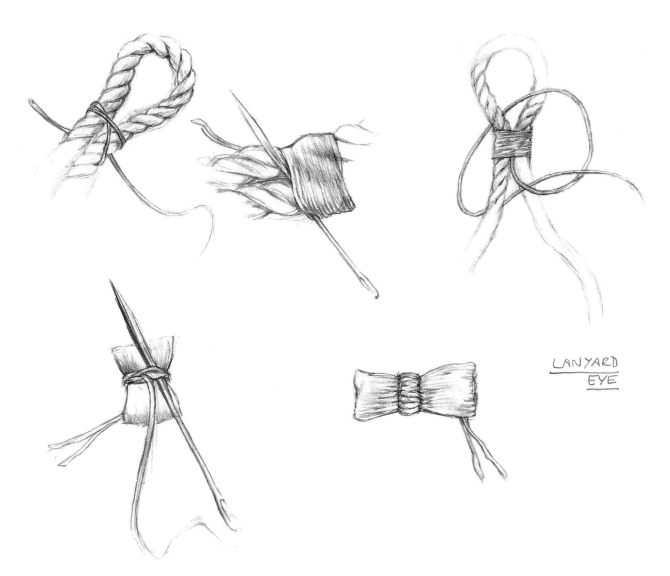

LANYARD
EYE

of the bag. Saw out just outside the mark-up as the bottom will fit better the harder
it is to insert.

The bottom should be fastened with two rows of close, diagonally-arranged
tacks. If the canvas edge is made to overlap the wooden piece, a canvas bottom can
be sewn in with a round seam.

My bag quickly fills with water but if you want to make yours tilt more quickly,
sew a lead sinker in under the rim, halfway between the lanyard cringles.

12

The tool wrapper

A worthy project, this. My odd assortment of fixed-head spanners had been rattling around noisily in the tool box, from Sète to Espalmador before I realised that their worn out plastic wrapper could be replaced by a canvas one.

Use at least 12 oz canvas, spread out your collection to determine what size wrapper is required. The figures given with the drawings are for nine pieces only.

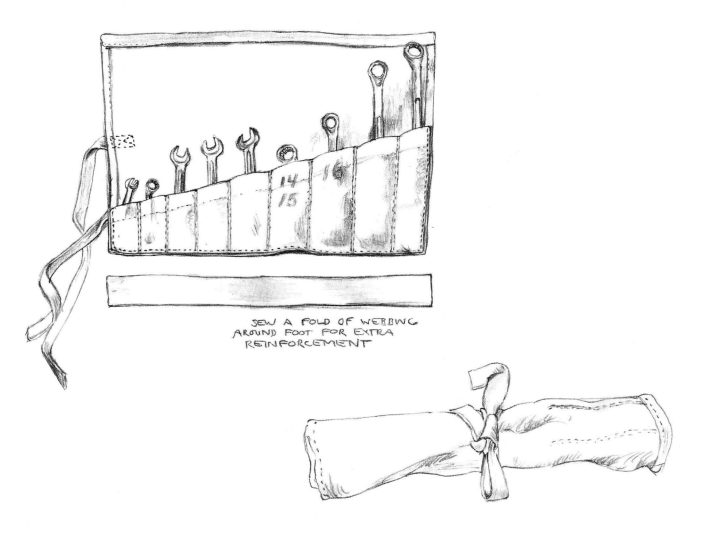

SEW A FOLD OF WEBBING
AROUND FOOT FOR EXTRA
REINFORCEMENT

On the main backing canvas, draw a half-inch (13 mm) tabling along the foot. Along the sides, mark up two half-inch tablings.

Cut a front piece the same width as the main one. Mark up a half-inch tabling all round, plus a 1½ in (3.8 cm) one inside the upper, sloping edge.

On the main piece, fold in and crease the outside half-inch, then fold it in once again on the inner pencil mark, tripling the cloth. Make a straight seam on the creased inside edge as shown by the two arrows in the drawing.

65

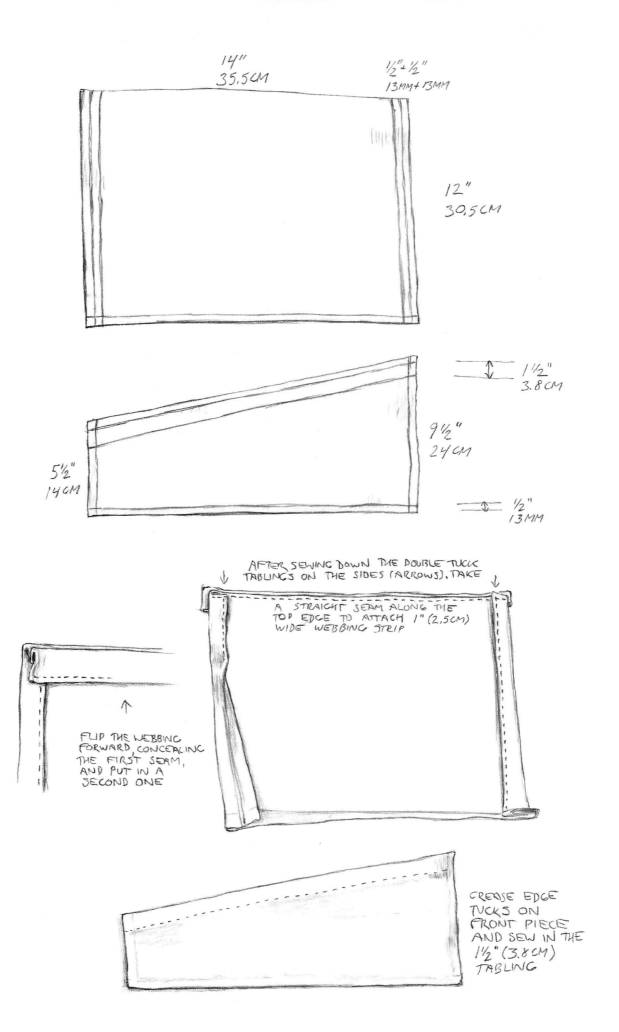

14"
35.5CM

½"+½"
13MM+13MM

12"
30.5CM

1½"
3.8CM

9½"
24CM

5½"
14CM

½"
13MM

AFTER SEWING DOWN THE DOUBLE TUCK
TABLINGS ON THE SIDES (ARROWS), TAKE
A STRAIGHT SEAM ALONG THE
TOP EDGE TO ATTACH 1" (2.5CM)
WIDE WEBBING STRIP

FLIP THE WEBBING
FORWARD, CONCEALING
THE FIRST SEAM,
AND PUT IN A
SECOND ONE

CREASE EDGE
TUCKS ON
FRONT PIECE
AND SEW IN THE
1½" (3.8CM)
TABLING

Next, position a length of webbing behind the top edge of the main piece and sew the two together with a straight seam. Flip the webbing forward as shown in the detail drawing and put in a second seam.

Taking the front piece, crease the tucks and sew in the tabling along the top.

Lay the front against the main piece, matching up the half-inch bottom tucks so that they are pressed in between, concealed and fixed with a straight seam through the four layers of canvas.

Sew the top piece on loosely so that there is a little extra cloth to make for bulkiness as the individual tool pockets are sewn in to suit your needs.

The bottom can be reinforced with webbing, and a length of soft webbing is a good choice for a tie-up.

Magazine pocket

On a boat you need to store everything in its place. Until I reached the eastern Mediterranean I had kept the ship's papers in a bulkhead pigeon-hole along with other documents. In view of the endless paper shuffling, the oft-used papers were moved to a handy pocket of their own.

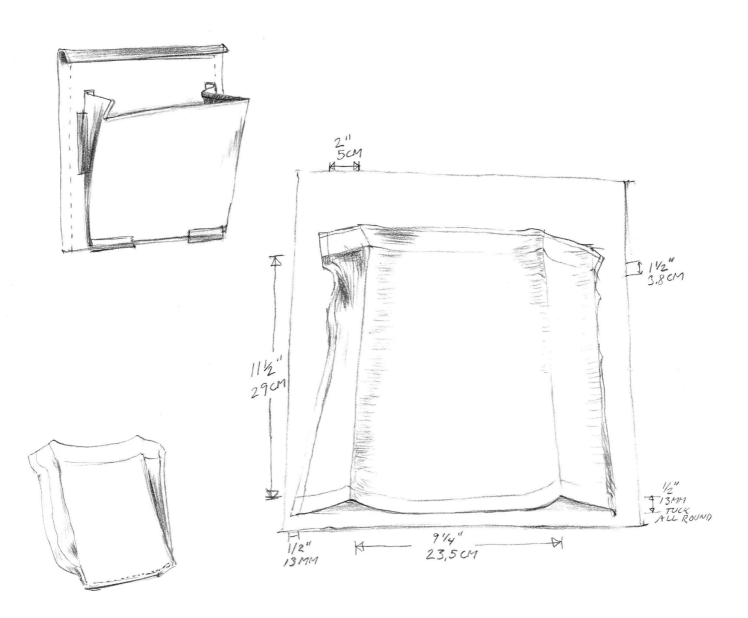

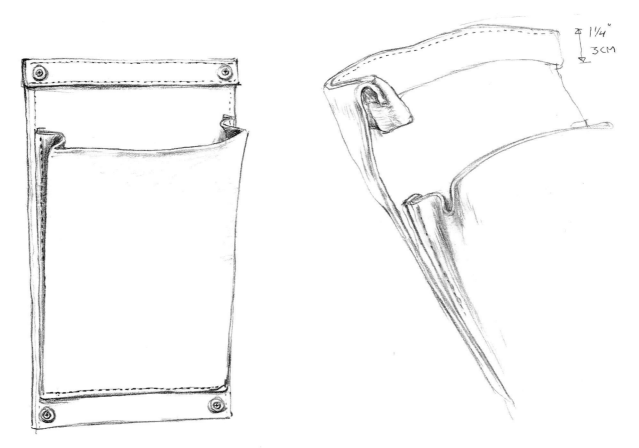

To make sure your dossier fits the outline given, make a paper dummy first, as shown, and try it.

To give the pocket substance, use heavy cotton canvas.

13
Flags

I set out in the *Moth* with a drawstring bag full of cotton flag bunting in red, white, blue, green, yellow and black.

On the eastern Frisian island of Langeoog I replaced the tabling of my light cotton national flag with cotton tape. A day of fresh winds over 'die Watten', the flat inter-tidal zone, blew the flag out of the cotton tape frame.

Flagmaking is a specialised skill. Lightness and unity of construction are necessary qualities. Any clumsy repair patch or addition will make the flag slat itself to pieces.

Use nylon or light cotton for manufacture, fitting pieces together with flat felled seams. Make the tabling by creasing and turning over the edges as shown in the drawing.

A heavier cotton tabling will stabilise the flag at the hoist end. Sew in loops for attachment, preferably with a swivel constituting the upper loop.

The *Moth*'s bag of bunting has not been transformed into as many flags as I had thought it would. For a reason, try counting the number of seams in the Greek flag.

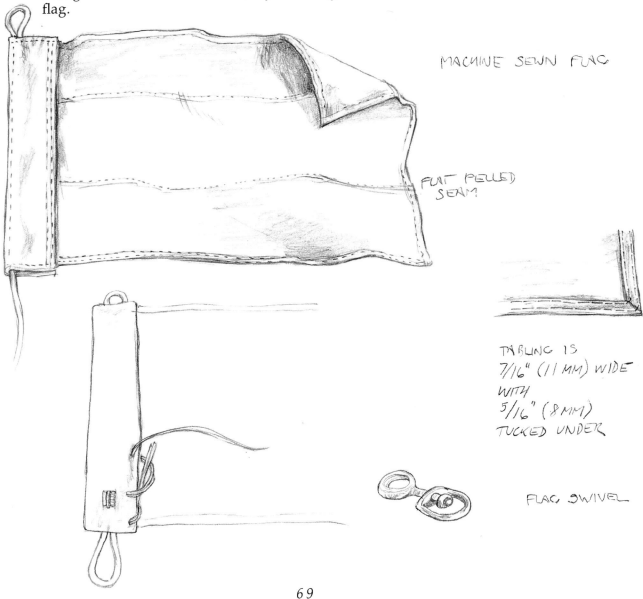

DOUBLED TABLING STRIP

MACHINE SEWN FLAG

FLAT FELLED SEAM

TABLING IS 7/16" (11 MM) WIDE WITH 5/16" (8 MM) TUCKED UNDER

FLAG SWIVEL

14
Fender covers

The heavy-duty, inflatable plastic fender is a marvel of durability but, going from harbour to harbour, the fender surface becomes scruffy and collects dirt. If the dirt amounts to grit, the fender will not just be a sorry sight but start to abrade against your topside varnish, paint or gelcoat.

A natty canvas duck cover will look better and can be taken off and scrubbed while the fender itself remains in pristine condition. I make mine in 8 oz canvas with an ample allowance, measuring from lanyard eye to lanyard eye, then adding 2 in (5 cm) plus a half inch (13 mm) tuck along the top and bottom.

To obtain the width of the workpiece, measure the girth of the fender when fully inflated. Add half an inch (13 mm) or 1 in (2.5 cm) in a large fender to this figure and lay it down on the canvas, flanked by the customary 1½ in (3.8 cm) plus half-inch (13 mm) tabling allowance.

The workpiece should be clearly marked with a carpenter's pencil before you turn it over and crease the 1½ in tabling. Put in a straight machine stitch near the edge of the second half-inch tuck to complete the tabling.

With the two tablings done, double the workpiece as shown in the diagonal drawing and put in another seam to join the edge of the two flaps. It should stop well short of the ends, as shown in the drawing. Double the seam.

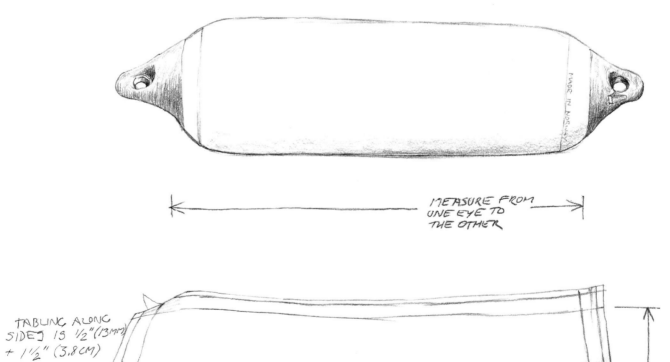

MEASURE FROM ONE EYE TO THE OTHER

TABLING ALONG SIDES IS ½" (13MM) + 1½" (3.8CM)

SAME MEASURE AS ABOVE

TOP AND BOTTOM TABLING IS ½" (13MM) ALONG THE EDGE AND 2" (5CM) FOR THE MAIN TUCK

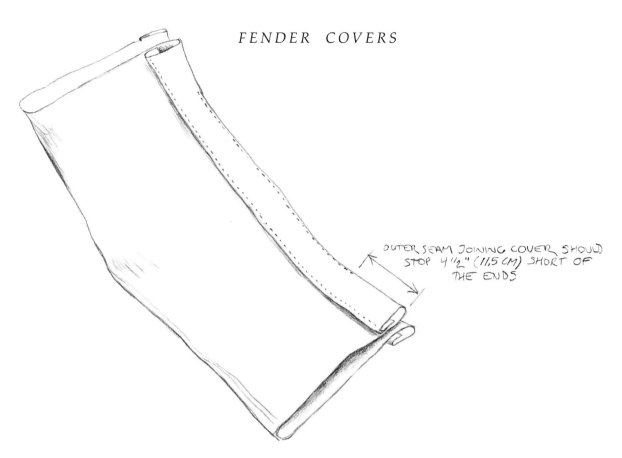

OUTER SEAM JOINING COVER SHOULD STOP 4½" (11,5 CM) SHORT OF THE ENDS

For the next step, look at the detail drawing.

The 2 in tabling is turned down, creased and marked along the middle where a straight seam is put in.

Before sewing in the half-inch tuck you will need a length of soft one eighth of an inch (3 mm) diameter drawstring, long enough to go twice around the cover. Tuck it in under the tabling and tie the two ends together as shown. Turn the workpiece right side out.

If, when fitting the covers, you find them to be skimpy, release a bit of air from the fender. You can always reflate again after the vest is on.

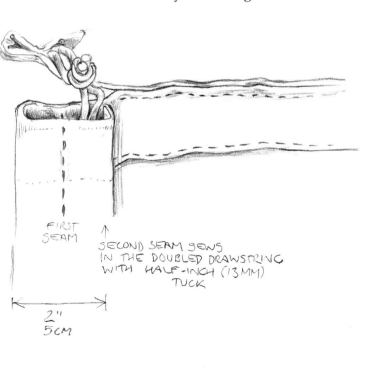

FIRST SEAM

SECOND SEAM SEWS IN THE DOUBLED DRAWSTRING WITH HALF-INCH (13 MM) TUCK

2"
5 CM

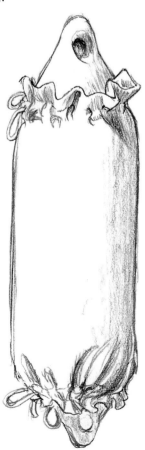

Should you be pining for a bit of hand seaming, the cover can be made with all flat seams, except for a running stitch in the middle of the 2 in tabling and a round seam to join the canvas flaps and make a cylinder shape.

Tie the drawstring with a shoelace knot and secure with an overhand knot of the two loops.

The washable fender cover, made of canvas or even of terry towelling, keeps the fender clean. However, when I tucked the *Moth* into Mykonos harbour in the Cyclades during a strong Meltemi burst, it soon became apparent that a clean fender is not enough. Sand from the Mykonos wastelands blew on the fender cover and began grinding against the side of the boat as it pressed against the quay. In a short while, the side of the boat became as dull as if it had been worked over vigorously with extremely coarse sandpaper.

The answer was to make a tabled canvas sheet, eyeletted in the upper corners, and suspend it from the rail, between boat side and fenders.

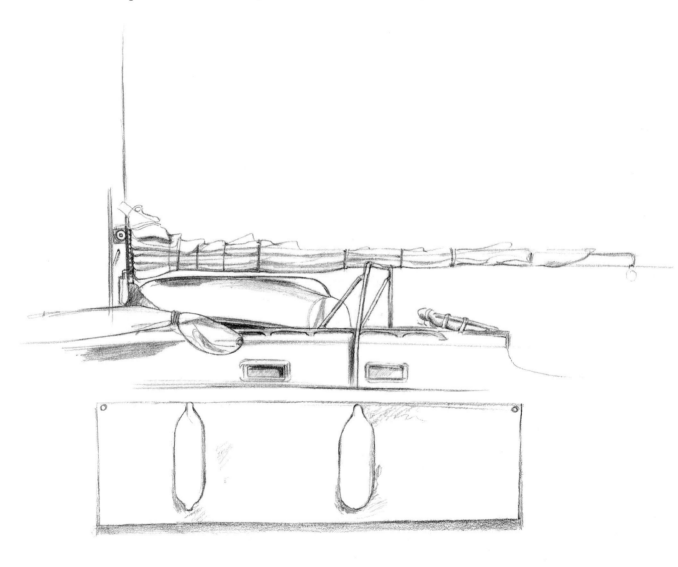

15
Wheel covers

As a parting gift to an Italian sailing family, the Ravasis, I made a proofed cover for the destroyer wheel on their Alpha 10.50. Don't ask me why the wheel needed a cover. It was the fashion on the Tiber to have one, that's all.

As the *Moth* was alongside their boat, I took two spare bits of canvas over and taped up front and back to the wheel consecutively, rubbing off a mark on the outside perimeter with a pencil, and cutting with several inches allowance outside.

The cut-out for the wheel attachment can be marked with a single circle for the centre and a 1½ in (3.8 cm) plus a half inch (13 mm) allowance on either side of a line running from the centre outwards. Start cutting on this line and proceed to take out the centre circle. Crease the 1½ in tablings and tuck under the half inch before taking a straight seam.

Find a spare length of webbing about three quarters of an inch (19 mm) wide and sew that all around the centre hole, with a straight seam near the inner edge.

Flip the workpiece over and pull the webbing over to the front so a seam can be taken along the opposite edge, concealing the first.

Turning again to the reverse side of the cloth, lay it down on the piece rubbed out for the front. Take a stitch around the top half, using staples or tape to keep the two cloths in alignment if need be.

Check the fit on the wheel. If satisfactory, you can add a second seam as shown in the small presser foot drawing, by folding over the sewing allowances and sewing parallel to the first seam, through three layers of cloth. The distance between the two is open to debate. Methin Balaban left only one sixteenth of an inch (0.6 mm) while I tend to allow almost a quarter of an inch (6.4 mm). Put a tabling in the unfinished edges of the cover.

Put in grommets, Velcro or zipper closures to hold the cover in place. The exact arrangement will depend on the attachment of the wheel.

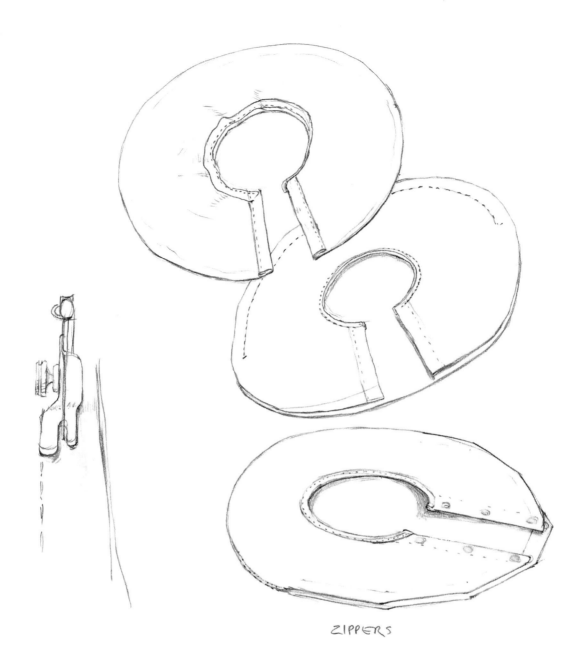

ZIPPERS

16
Binnacle and odd covers

After I had made the wheel cover for the Ravasis, the binnacle looked rather forlorn. The compass on their boat was exposed and needed protection much more than the wheel.

I made no measurements but went ahead with a method that I began using when travelling between Turkey and Egypt. It was inspired by breathing the oriental air, but has proved very useful ever since.

You forget about measurements and simply lay wrapping paper or the proposed material over the object to be covered. In the case of a binnacle, there will of course be creases but they can be summed up in main ones. When I folded the material into an overlap that was small at the centre but wide at the sides, the material fitted the compass dome.

Use a carpenter's pencil to mark the extent of the overlap of the doubled cloth, as well as how far back the tripled cloth extends.

Laying the marked up cloth out flat, there is a pattern plainly marked, as shown by the bold lines in the drawing. Add a 1 in (2.5 cm) sewing allowance to one side and a half-inch (13 mm) to the other. In addition, trace a half-inch allowance outside the circle that marks the top of the binnacle pedestal.

Cut out the two halves and lay the piece with the half-inch allowance on top of the one with 1 in marked.

Put in a straight seam to join them, then fold the wider allowance over the shorter, lay the tripled part against the main workpiece and put in a second straight seam.

Lay another piece of canvas against the binnacle pedestal and determine how

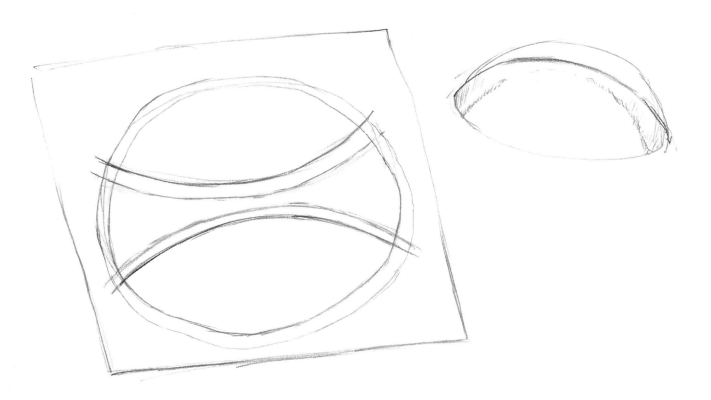

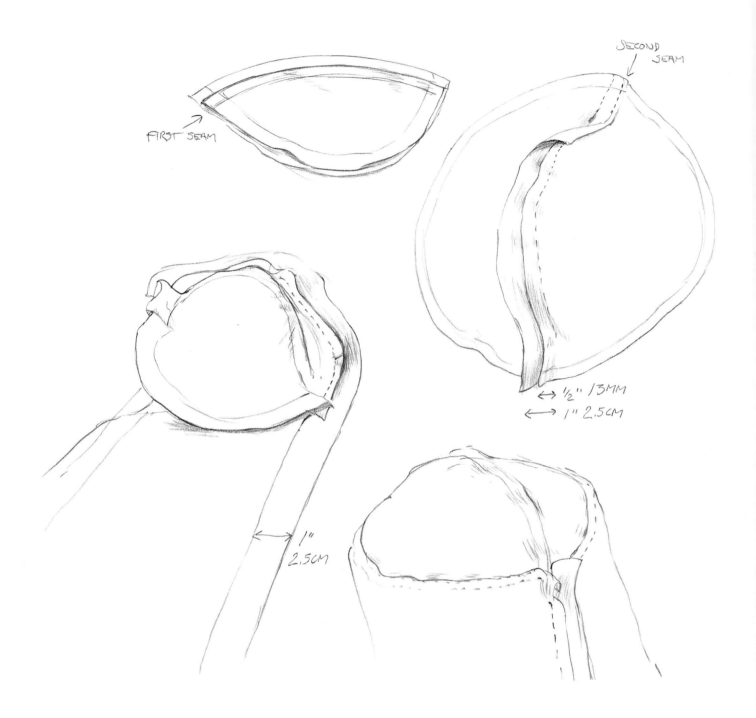

far down you want the cover to extend. Mark a 1 in (2.5 cm) wide allowance at the top and leave a couple of extra inches at the bottom.

Marking on the reverse side of the dome, lay the half-inch allowance in the top piece against the 1 in allowance marked on the upper edge of the body strip – which should be several inches longer than the circumference of the dome.

Make a straight seam first to join the pieces (in exactly the same way as when joining the first two pieces to form the dome) and a second one after the wider allowance has been folded over the shorter one.

When you have sewn right around the dome, the ends of the body piece will meet. Cut the two edges to the same inch and half-inch allowance and put in your third double seam. Thus, all seams except the bottom tabling will be flat felled seams.

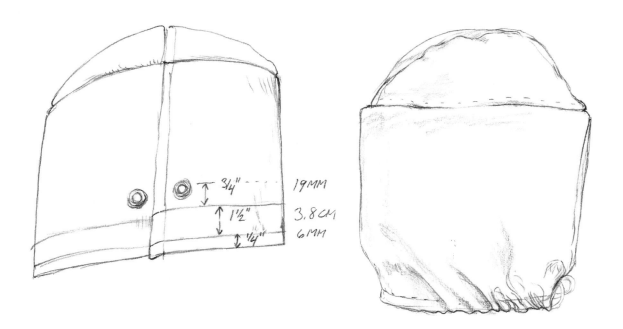

Mark up the bottom tabling as shown by the drawing and put in two small grommets on either side of the main seam.

Crease and fold along the pencil lines and sew in the tuck to the inside of the cover, not forgetting to slip a drawstring into the tabling.

The 'rough cut-out' method used can be applied to just about any difficult-to-measure object on board that needs to be covered.

17

Piston hank lacing

Of all the shipboard tasks, few have as satisfying a nature as the fitting or replacement of piston hanks for the headsail luff.

Also, having tried zipper luffs, clips and grooved profiles, I am hard put to name a better way of bending on a headsail in a tidy, bluewater way.

The charm of putting in a hank is of the same nature as handseaming. You balance your handiwork, in this instance by making three separate twine lacings that, if you have put in the right tension, will in the end come out in perfect balance, poising the hank out firmly from the luff.

The size of hanks ranges from one and a quarter inches (3.2 cm) long to the large fist-size ones you find on traditional schooners.

For yachts, bronze has a better feel but also more weight than stainless steel and other alternatives.

The durability of the bronze hanks is such that you may often pass the hanks of an old sail over to a new one, especially if the spring inside has been kept lively by a freshwater rinse and a drop of oil now and again. If the part that encircles the wire is worn down by more than a third of its thickness, new hanks should be substituted.

The work calls for a seaming palm, heavy duty waxed polyester twine, a No.14½ needle and a lump of beeswax. Thread a generous fathom of twine, double and twist. Fix the twist by drawing the twine over the beeswax.

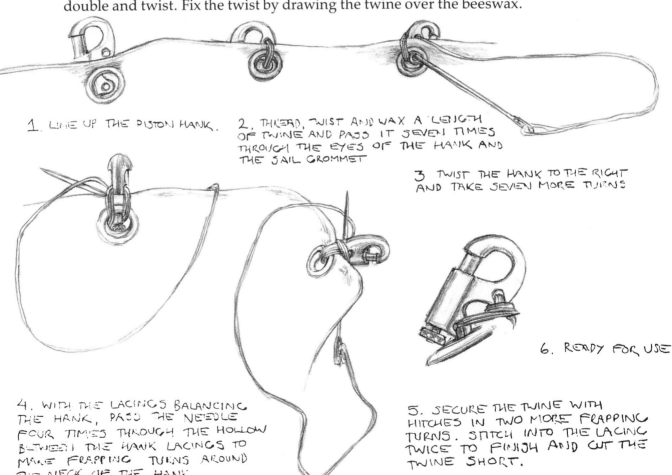

1. LINE UP THE PISTON HANK.

2. THREAD, TWIST AND WAX A LENGTH OF TWINE AND PASS IT SEVEN TIMES THROUGH THE EYES OF THE HANK AND THE SAIL GROMMET

3. TWIST THE HANK TO THE RIGHT AND TAKE SEVEN MORE TURNS

4. WITH THE LACINGS BALANCING THE HANK, PASS THE NEEDLE FOUR TIMES THROUGH THE HOLLOW BETWEEN THE HANK LACINGS TO MAKE FRAPPING TURNS AROUND THE NECK OF THE HANK

5. SECURE THE TWINE WITH HITCHES IN TWO MORE FRAPPING TURNS. STITCH INTO THE LACING TWICE TO FINISH AND CUT THE TWINE SHORT.

6. READY FOR USE

18
Round cushions

To make a round cushion, suitable for a sailmaker's bench or any round seat, draw up the size on 10 oz canvas as shown by the solid line in the mark-up drawing, going by the size of the compressed foam pad that you are going to stuff it with.

Draw an outside dotted line at half the thickness of the foam pad. Draw a final outside line another half-inch (13 mm) wide of the second line.

Staple the canvas to another piece of the same weight and put in a straight machine seam along the middle mark-up line.

Leave a 10 in (25 cm) opening on one side. Cut along the far outside line and turn the work right side out.

Stuff the cushion inside and close the opening with a neat hand stitch.

Tie-down ribbons can also be added.

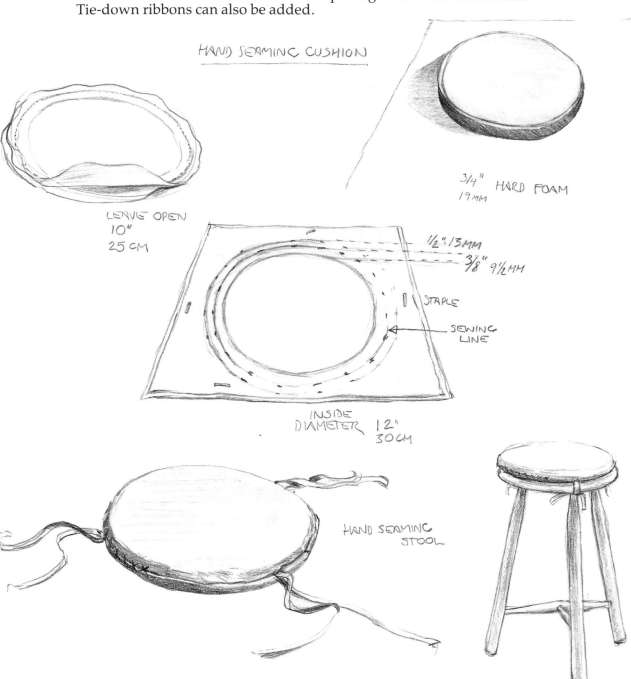

HAND SEAMING CUSHION

LEAVE OPEN
10"
25 CM

3/4" HARD FOAM
19 MM

1/2" 13 MM
3/8" 9½ MM

STAPLE

SEWING LINE

INSIDE DIAMETER 12"
30 CM

HAND SEAMING STOOL

19

Square cushions

To make a comfortable shipboard cushion, try to find a piece of foam 1 in (5 cm) thick and as firm as possible.

For seagoing use, a closed-cell foam is the ideal cushion filler but if hard to find, use compressed polyurethane foam. Another kind of water-proofing consists of using vinyl as cover material but stable cotton canvas is softer on eye and hand.

To cut foam to size, use a sharp, serrated knife, making a sawing motion.

Measure up two identical pieces of 10 oz canvas – of 13½ in × 19 in (34 cm × 48 cm) in this example – allowing for 1 in (2.5 cm) outside borders.

You will also need a strip 2 in (5 cm) wide plus 1 in (2.5 cm) seaming allowances on either side. The length for the size I have given here should be 40 in (102 cm) but there is no need to spoil a good bolt of canvas if you have shorter pieces that can be sewn together as shown in the drawing.

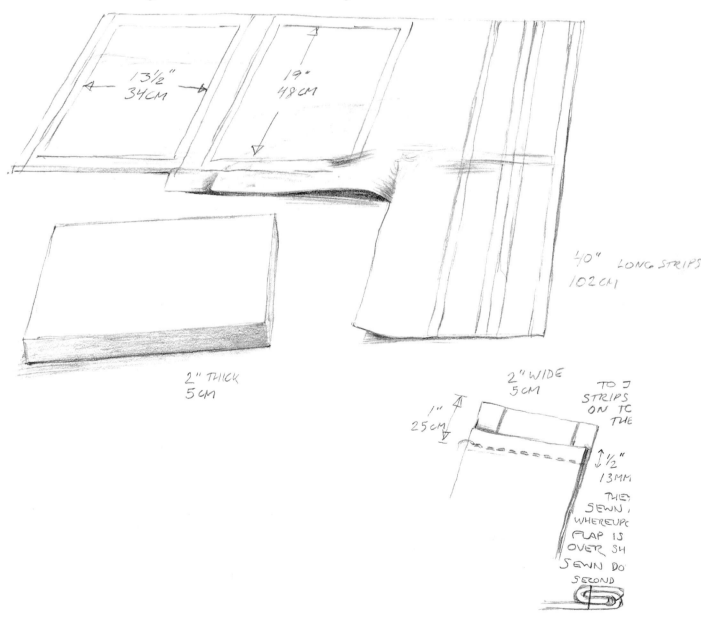

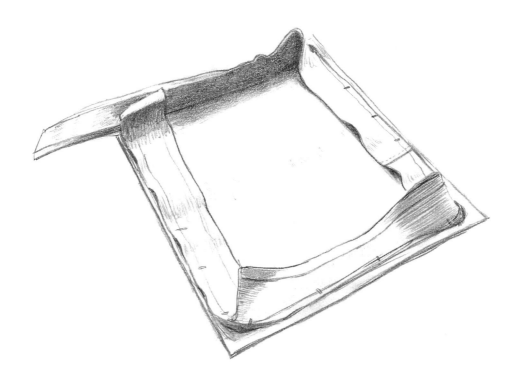

Tack the border strip provisionally to one side piece as shown in the drawing. The one inch border allowance should overlap precisely so the pencil lines coincide. If tacks or pins are put in at right angles to the seam mark-up, a straight seam can be taken without removing them – but go gently. Sew right around and remove the tacks.

In similar fashion, sew the other half to the strip, leaving one end open to turn the cushion cover inside out, add a zipper, and stuff in the cushion.

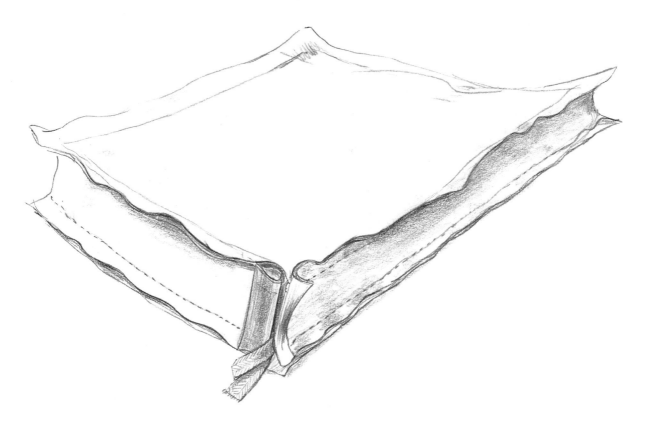

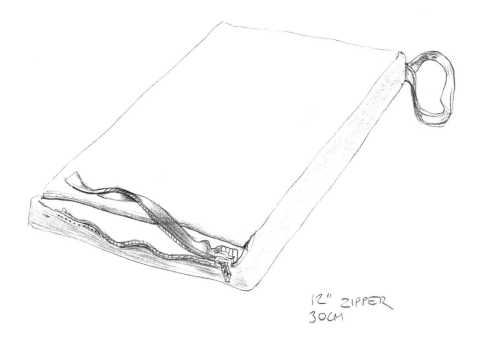

12" ZIPPER
30CM

In Turkey, there is a simpler way. Even Methin Balaban stoops to it. You lay two pieces of canvas back to back, or fold two edges of one piece if that is more convenient, and make a straight stitch along a line determined by a generous outline of a cushion filler plus half the thickness of the filler material. Allow for spare cloth all around and an aperture to slip in the cushion.

The square shape is achieved by sewing in the corners as shown in the drawing. Turn the finished cover right side out, slip in the cushion and hand sew the aperture closed with a round seam.

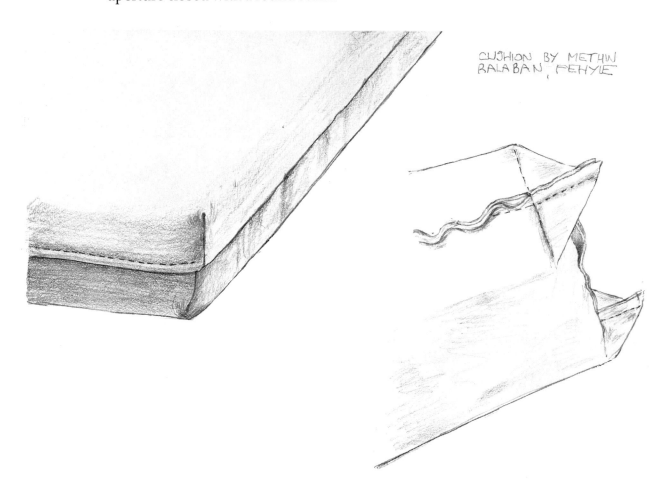

CUSHION BY METHIN
BALABAN, FEHYIE

20
The bosun's chair

It is in the nature of woven canvas that a piece cut out of it requires turning over twice at the edges in order to make a usable flat piece that does not unravel.

The doubled edge, which is called the tabling, makes a good anchorage for roping or eyelets and steadies the canvas.

Among the rules of thumb that guide the width of canvas tabling, I have adopted one that calls for a 1½ in (3.8 cm) wide tabling, with an inside tuck of half an inch (13 mm).

The three-layer drawing shows how the tucks for the tabling are made. For guidelines, mark up 12 oz canvas as in the chair materials drawing. A batten or ruler is useful in joining measurement points. A T-square can also be handy.

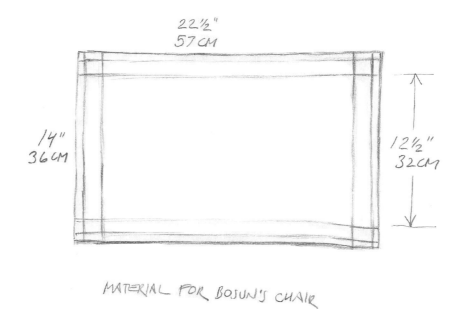

MATERIAL FOR BOSUN'S CHAIR

Cut the material to the outside measurements. Fold in along the pencil lines and crease along the edges with the back of a clasp knife blade so the doubled tabling lies well against the canvas as a flat hand seam or a straight machine stitch is taken ³⁄₃₂ in (2.5 mm) inside the doubled edge.

Take 16 ft (4 m) of first-class three-strand Dacron or polypropylene measuring half an inch (12 mm) or more in diameter according to the weight of people who will use the chair. Dacron webbing is also an alternative although the result would be just a rope chair.

Centre the rope along the far, long side of the canvas seat.

Take a No.14½ needle with a blunt point and thread, double, twist and wax a fathom of heavy polyester seaming twine. With the rope pressed against the canvas – which can be tensioned from the right with a canvas hook – start putting in a roping stitch as shown by the drawings opposite, going from left to right clean under the top strand. The first few stitches and the last should be doubled for security. All should be hove home tight, preferably with a few turns around a thumb protector on a heavy-duty seaming palm.

Before joining the ends of the rope for roping to the other long end of the seat, you have a choice between a long or short splice. The long splice is neater and better suited to roping work, but the short splice is stronger.

My preference is for the long splice, but be sure to practise a couple of times if you have not made one before.

Rope in the spliced part securely, doubling back the hand seam all along the canvas.

Arrange the rope so that it forms two loops with an even pull on all four corners of the canvas seat.

Thread, double, twist and wax another length of heavy seaming twine and seize the doubled eye as in the drawings on page 86, starting by stitching through a couple of times or locking in the end carefully as the first turns are taken. With enough turns to equal the diameter of the rope, stitch the needle down through the eye formed, back up between the ropes and into the eye made by the twine. Make two of these hitches, heaving home tight every time. Stitch through several times to finish, before cutting.

A neater alternative is to end by stitching riding turns around the cross turns taken earlier.

Tie a halyard into your flying carpet. I prefer to go aloft on an all-rope halyard

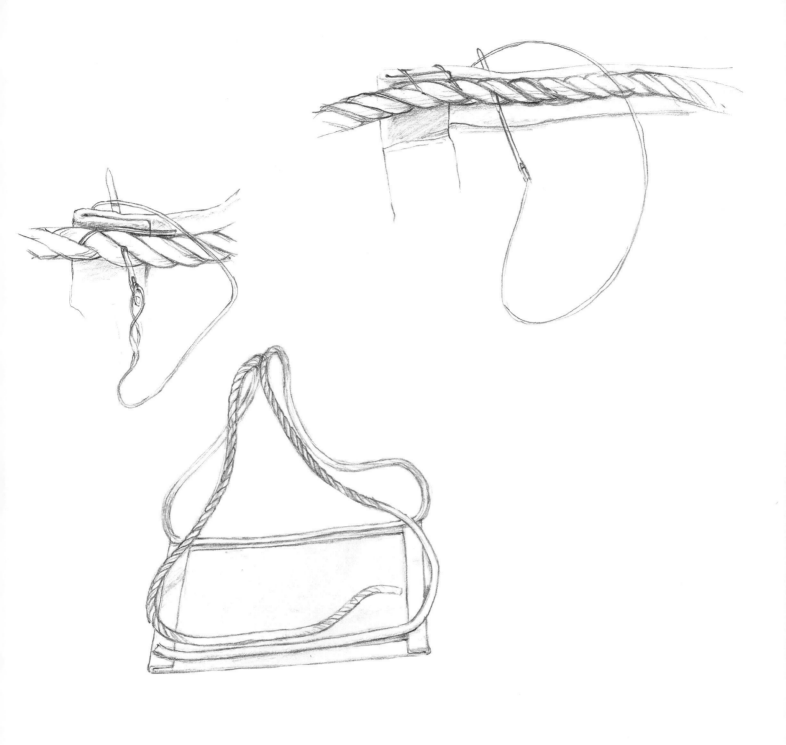
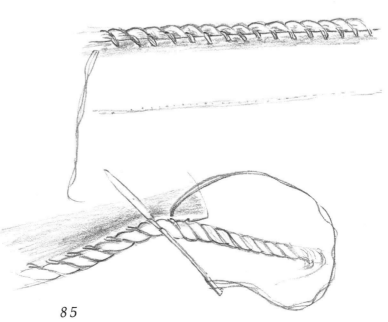

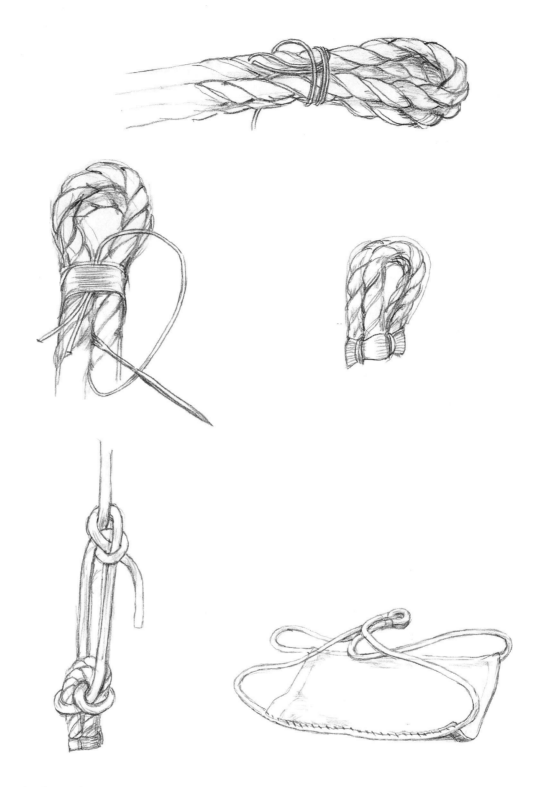

which can be secured to the eye of the bosun's chair with the bowline shown in the drawing, well drawn home and settled.

If you have to use a wire halyard, do not rely simply on the shackle or snap shackle at the end. With your life and limb at stake, take the end of the wire through the eye on the bosun's chair to form a clove hitch lashing before the end is shackled to the standing part.

Make a last inspection of your handiwork and jump heavily into the chair a couple of times at low altitude to make sure it will not fail you at the top of the mast.

21
The mainsail cover

On any latitude, a mainsail cover is essential for protecting the key sail against pollutant particles and the rays of the sun. If you replace an existing, well-fitting cover, the dimensions can be taken from that. Otherwise, you should fold up the main on the boom in the customary way and arm yourself with a tape measure.

The most important measure is taken diagonally around the bulkiest part of the

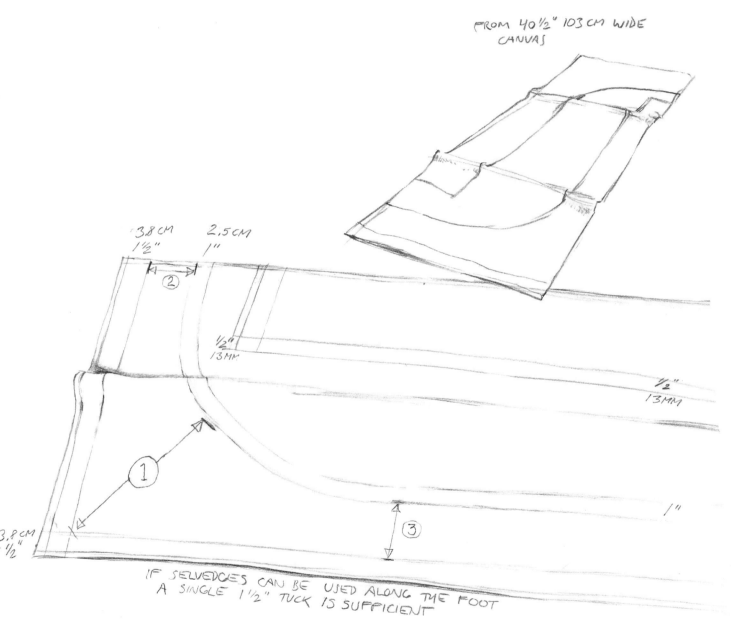

FROM 40½" 103 CM WIDE
CANVAS

3.8 CM
1½"

2.5 CM
1"

②

½"
13 MM

½"
13 MM

①

3.8 CM
1½"

③

1"

IF SELVEDGES CAN BE USED ALONG THE FOOT
A SINGLE 1½" TUCK IS SUFFICIENT

OTHERWISE, THE OUTER, ½".13MM
TUCK SHOULD ALSO BE DRAWN
UP AND THE FOOT FOLDED
TWICE

sail and right around the mast to the bottom of a line projecting forward from the nether side of the boom.

The second measurement is taken higher up on the mast where the bulk of the sail reaches its minimum. A third measurement belongs to the point where the sail on the boom has tapered down to an even line.

Knowing these measurements, and the distance between them, the material can be marked up with chalk or carpenter's pencil.

The choice in material is between proofed cotton canvas and synthetics. In terms of looks and feel the cotton is clearly more attractive but you can get away with a lighter weight in synthetics, a very obvious advantage in a large cover at least.

The cover I made in Alicante was of white unresinated synthetic sail cloth material and wonderfully light to handle. It is not proof against rain or spray but it soaks up the sunrays which would otherwise weaken the main.

Mark up the material, if possible economising by letting the two sides of the cover oppose one another diagonally on a single length of cloth. Be sure to leave the recommended sewing allowances and tablings enough space outside the mere dimensions of the cover.

Note that the upper, curved part of one is marked up with a 1 in border, while the opposing one only has a half-inch wide one.

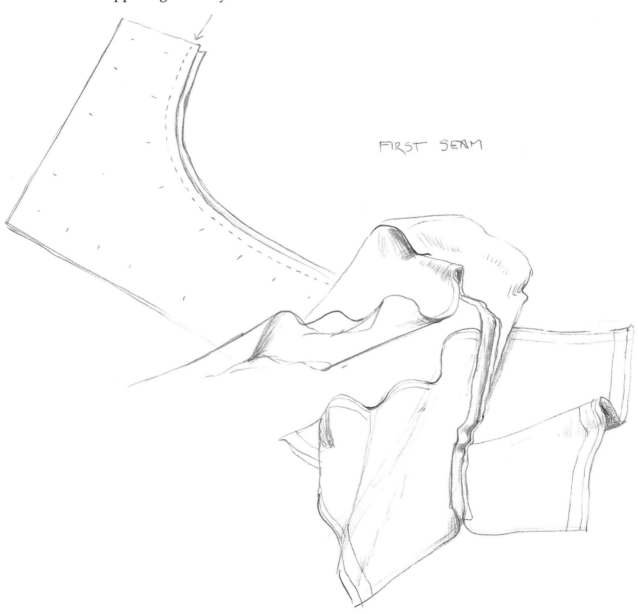

FIRST SEAM

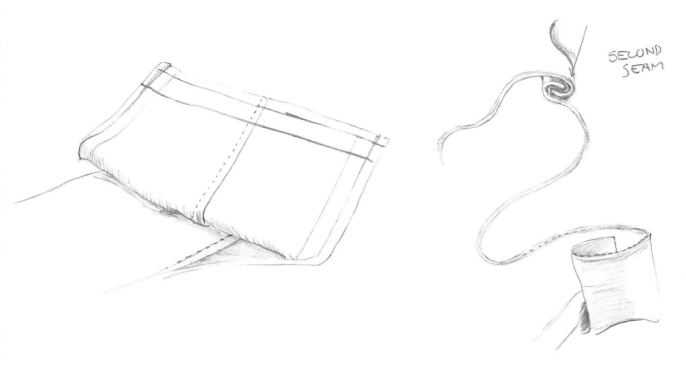

After cutting out, lay the two halves on top of one another, the one with the inch-wide allowance underneath. If need be, put a couple of staples through the doubled cloth to keep the two pieces in their exact position as you start running a straight machine stitch along the half-inch mark-up. The seam should also coincide with the 1 in marking underneath. Run the seam right back to the outhaul end of the cover.

Tuck the half-inch wide lip out to lie against the canvas and crease the 1 in flap over it. The second seam is taken close to the doubled edge of this fold-over. With the two halves of the cover flipped apart, sew right back to the outhaul end again.

Before turning in and creasing down the tabling along the front and foot of the cover, fit the cover on to the sail on the boom, if possible. This final fitting makes all the difference between a fitted suit and one fashioned on a tailor's dummy.

The front should just barely come together and the foot should be a few inches short, allowing air to circulate upwards into the sometimes damp sail.

Lace-up lines or spur teeth grommets should be put into the front tabling at 10 in intervals, one opposite the other.

For a clean look, make a flap the length of the front and sufficiently wide to cover the lace-up. Sew it into the left side of the front, 1½ in (3.8 cm) from the edge.

Sew a length of soft webbing to the back of the cover so it can be taken right around twice to secure the top collar.

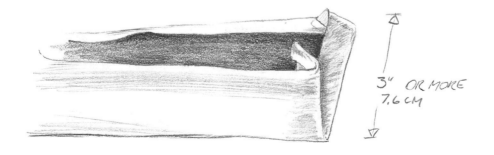

1½"

SOFT WEBBING

3CM   1¼"

LACE POINTS
EVERY 10"
25CM

90

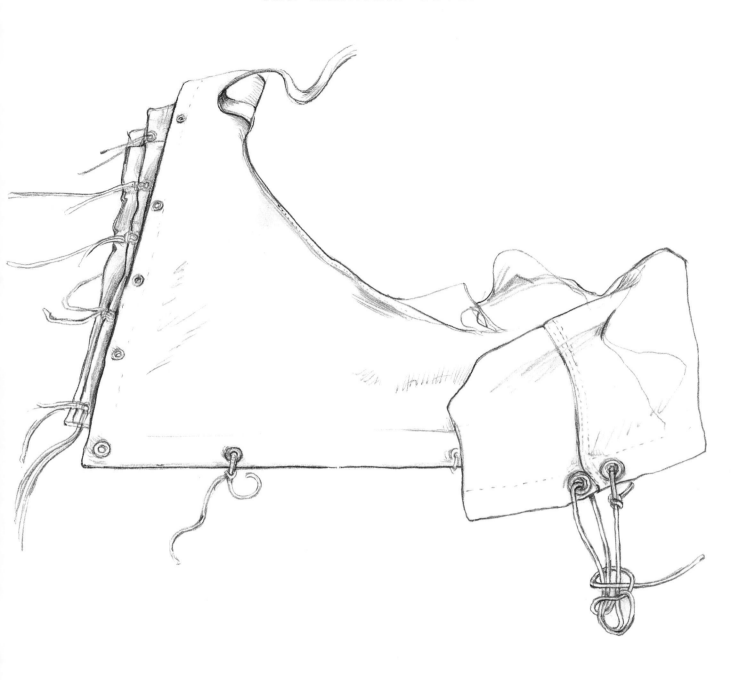

Along the foot, space the grommets or lace-up lines at fathom or closer intervals.

Put in double grommets at the outhaul end of the cover to allow for a clean running triple line purchase.

Clove hitch the end over the purchase lines to finish.

Lace up starting from the front. The last tensioning is made on the triple purchase, making the turnover flat felled seam on top of the cover rise into a well-fitting ridge.

22

The canvas hammock

On overland trips from the Corsican hills to the placid shore of the Sea of Galilee, I used a canvas hammock strung up between two trees for my repose and never spent a more comfortable night.

Aboard, the hammock has seen use slung between the spinnaker pole ring on the mast and the headstay, a retreat for reading.

The length recommended here is for a 6-foot person and the width has a little to do with the full use of a bolt of canvas. If possible, use the 1 m plus width that most canvas comes in as this has a non-fraying selvedge and will only require a single tuck at the tabling.

Mark up 10 or 12 oz canvas with a carpenter's pencil and cut to outside dimensions, allowing for tablings. Lay the piece face down on a flat surface or across your knee and proceed to put hard creases along the pencil lines with the back of a knife blade.

Sew down the double fold or selvedge with a straight or zig-zag machine stitch right on the inside edge. If hand seaming, a flat seam is used all around.

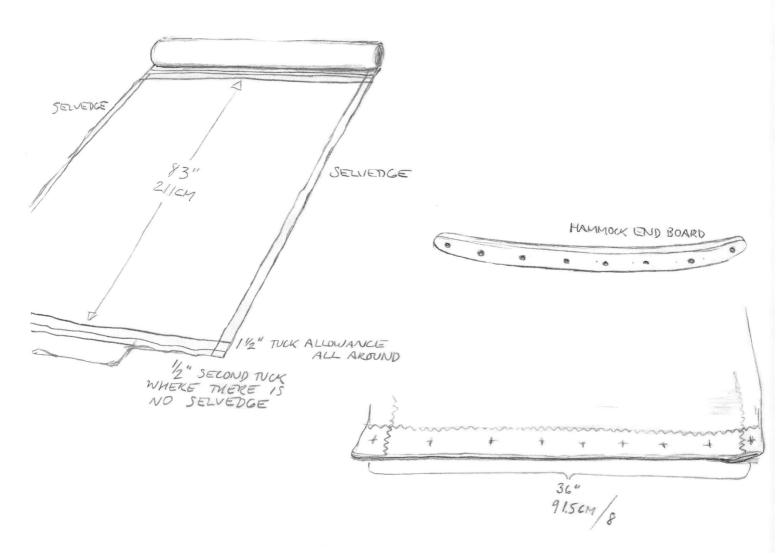

SELVEDGE

SELVEDGE

83"
211CM

HAMMOCK END BOARD

1½" TUCK ALLOWANCE
ALL AROUND

½" SECOND TUCK
WHERE THERE IS
NO SELVEDGE

36"
91.5CM /8

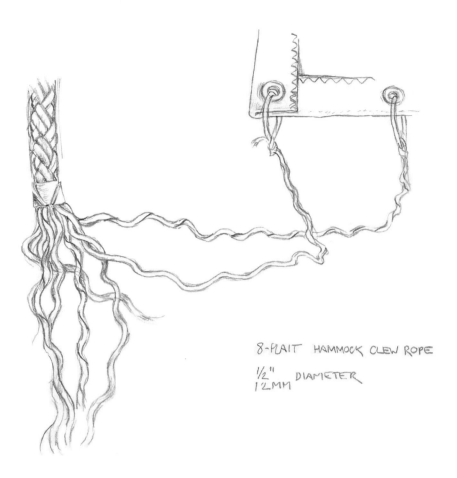

8-PLAIT HAMMOCK CLEW ROPE

½" DIAMETER
12MM

Measure up the short ends and put in eight neatly spaced No.1 spur teeth grommets. Pass a seizing fathom from the end of an 8-plait Dacron line and unwind the strands, inserting equal tension bowlines through the grommets with the ends of the strands.

For a flatter hammock, fashion two end boards with eight holes drilled to accommodate the clew ropes at equal spacing from the grommet holes. A slight crescent curve makes the hammock even more inviting.

23
The canvas dodger

As its name implies, a dodger is used as a dodge, usually against inclement weather. On bluewater boats it is also a popular method of displaying the name or number of the boat for easy identification. The *Moth* has a matching pair on either

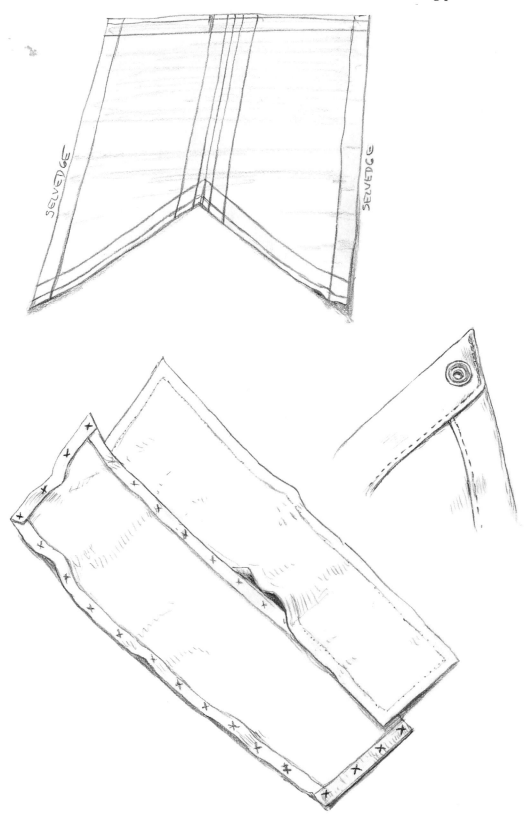

side of the rather shallow cockpit. The canvas keeps out spray and tempers the gusts in stormy weather. At port, it makes the cockpit more comfortable.

Use any sturdy canvas, if possible matching sprayhood and sail cover. The size needed depends on the boat and only on-the-spot measurement will do. Measure off the square bordered by the stern pulpit, the life line, the first stanchion, and the rail of the boat. Note down any particulars, such as the best placing of lacing eyelets and if the winch handle needs a hole to swing.

If possible, mark up two strips back-to-back, as shown, to make full use of the canvas and two non-fraying selvedges. All sides need to be marked for a 1½ in (3.8 cm) wide tabling with an extra tucking allowance of half an inch (13 mm). The latter is not needed along selvedges.

Note that the two pieces are not identical, but mirror images. Cut them apart if the mark-up has been made on a single piece, and lay them with the marked-up side down as you put in a hard crease along the double and single pencil lines.

Fold the tabling along the canvas and, with the half-inch allowance tucked underneath, sew it down with a single machine seam at the doubled edge, right around.

The resulting dodgers should be identical when laid together front-to-front, as in the drawing. The sides with the tabling are the reverse sides and on these the spur teeth grommet holes can be marked up, preferably on board the boat to place them in the most effective lacing spots.

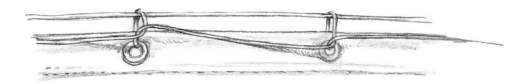

Put in the grommets from the reverse, tabled side, as this will show up their brassy side. Lace up the dodgers with a marline hitch and enjoy the arboreal feeling these shelters lend to a cockpit.

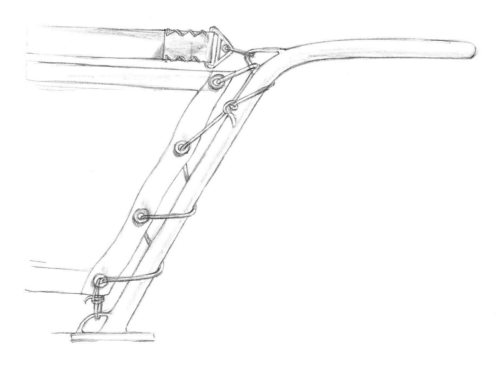

24
The sea anchor

The canvas sea anchor has much in common with a parachute. Both are often squared off circles with a hole at their centres for directional stability as a body pulls at them from lines attached around their outside edges. In heavy weather, the anchor can be streamed from the quarter or another convenient point under bare poles, keeping the boat at a comfortable angle and under some measure of control. Ideally, that is. Opinion differs widely on whether you should stream a succession of sea anchors, whether the material should be porous, whether, indeed, they are any good at all.

Any arrangement should be geared to your boat. I offer the following project as a starting point.

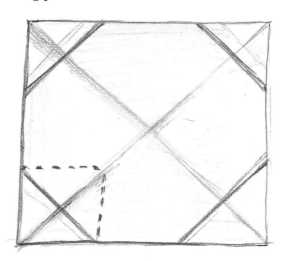

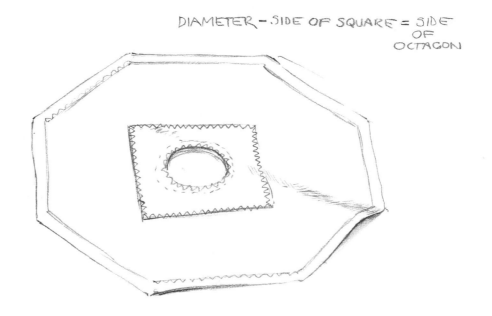

DIAMETER – SIDE OF SQUARE = SIDE OF OCTAGON

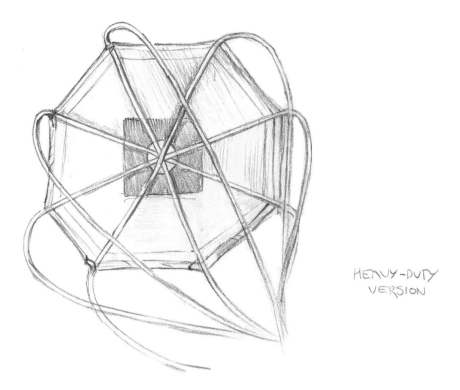

HEAVY-DUTY
VERSION

The useful size varies, but for a modern, 30-foot fin keeler you should start with a 1 m² or 40 in of material.

Heavy, 12 oz canvas is the traditional sea anchor material but lately this has been replaced by heavily reinforced vinyl of the type used as covers on long-distance lorries and trailers. This is very strong and does not rot, mildew or absorb water.

Make sure you have an even-sided square. Measure off the diameter and subtract from it the length of the side of the square. This gives the length of the side when the square is cut up to make an octagon.

Turn one corner of the square in along the diameter and make a crease or grease crayon mark when the outside fold reaches the measure you have calculated for the side of the octagon.

Measure and mark this distance all around and cut off the four corners accordingly. Cut a hole in the centre 2 in (5 cm) in diameter. Cut a reinforcement patch that fits around the hole. Trace off the outline and sew it in securely with a straight or zig-zag machine stitch (the hand seaming version is given later). A little oil on the lower tarpaulin surface helps to run it through the machine more smoothly.

Mark up and fold over a 1½ in (4 cm) wide tabling along the outside edges, sew down the inside edge with a zig-zag stitch if possible, tucking a 5/16 of an inch (8 mm) diameter rope in as you go along, letting it form a loop at each corner. Next, sew the rope snugly into the fold using a single presser foot on the sewing machine. If the space between presser foot and feeder is sufficient on your machine, also take a seam right around on top of the rope. Otherwise, double, twist and use a fathom of twine on a No. 15 sailmaker's needle and seize the rope in with a few stitches on either side of the loops. These loops should be seized together at the base anyway so the strain on the sea anchor is evenly distributed.

If you want to hand sew the anchor, use a roping stitch all around, allowing for the loops as you go along. Drop the centre reinforcement patch in favour of roping sewn into the centre cut-out.

Make up four 160-inch lines (400 cm). Double them and seize the loops together.

The ends are bowlined to the eight 'ears' on the sea anchor. Put a line through the eye where these lanyards come together and the anchor is ready for launching.

If you anticipate heavy and frequent use for the anchor, the lanyards can be arranged differently, sewn right across the sea anchor for maximum strength.

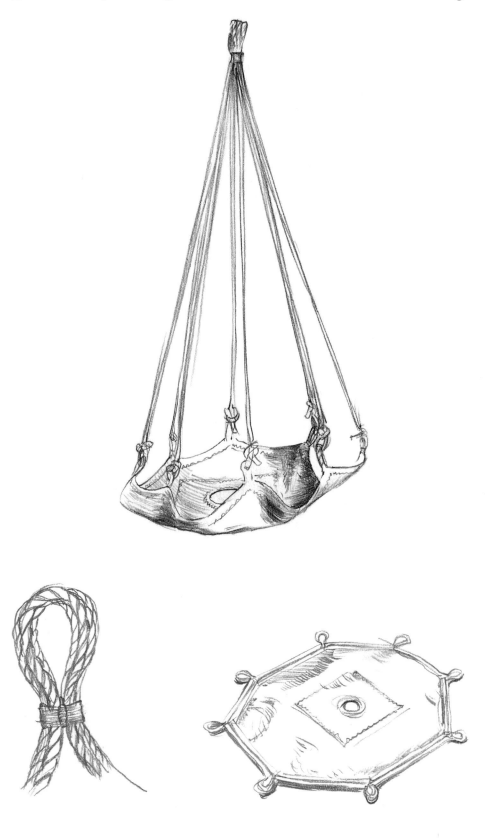

25
Sprayhood

To make a well-fitting sprayhood is as great a challenge as making a sail and will reflect your standard of canvaswork even at dockside. The hood itself has become a standard feature, having almost all the advantages of a fixed doghouse without the drawbacks of permanent tophamper.

The most common flaw that develops in a sprayhood is the appearance of cracks in the plastic window material, where the window has been folded or creased. Careful handling, i.e. gently folding in the window when the hood is lowered, rather than just dropping the hood, will much prolong its life, as will a regular freshwater rinse.

Should the window still go first, it can be replaced according to the directions that follow, but first we'll examine the making of a new sprayhood.

As with other items of on-board canvas, a well-fitting old one can be used as a template for a new one. Otherwise, the measurements are taken from the bows, set up with steadying twine in the position you have chosen over the companion-way.

If you are making an arrangement from scratch, the classic model would consist of two hoops, as in the replacement sprayhood for the *Moth* that I have sketched. The measurement is for a front piece, a 'roof' piece, and two small triangular pieces of canvas on either side with which to pull the hood up. Aluminium hoops can be shaped easily but also bend out of shape when used as a handhold. Stainless steel hoops are much better but have to be specially made.

Measure the length of the hoops from pivot point to pivot point, then take the length of the semicircle at which it is attached to the deck. Also measure the middle lines marked by dotting in the drawing.

By halving the dotted pivot to pivot measurements, find the centre or amidship position on the hood. Take the halfway figure and divide it by three to establish two points between the centre and the pivot at which width measurements can be taken in both directions.

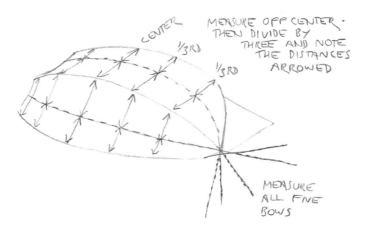

With these measurements to hand, lay down the dimensions of the sprayhood on crosshatched paper, to scale. Strike an even circle along the reference points noted.

For a realistic trial of your mini-hood, trace it off and tape together at the edges to see if it has the general appearance of the hood you want on your boat.

Care is important in the taking of the measurements and it is essential when striking them out full scale on canvas.

The choice in material is between the feel (and comparative scarcity!) of high quality proofed cotton canvas and a synthetic or mixture of both. I would favour a light, blended material.

Use a carpenter's pencil to mark up white canvas and a white crayon to mark up blue or green material. Lay down the dimensions as on paper, but full scale this time. Allow plenty of spare material at the lower end of the front piece and give it half an inch (13 mm) sewing allowance at the top end.

The roof part should have a full inch allowance towards the front and back.

The triangular side pieces should be measured and cut out with an extra tabling allowance of 1½ in + ½ in (3.8 cm + 13 mm) all around except on the side which joins the sprayhood which only needs a half-inch wide allowance.

Mark up on opposite sides so you'll get two mirror image pieces.

Sprayhood Window

Adding a window to the sprayhood is best done before the front panel is joined to the rest. Transparent material for the job is sold by many canvas supply stores in fixed sizes. Save the half you may not use immediately as it will come in handy when replacing the cracked window in a couple of years' time – the sprayhood itself should last longer.

The size and placement of the window requires some consideration as it will affect the appearance of your boat. My own view is that the soaring curves of the canvas should not be imitated in the window outlines. A simple, squared window, à la old Broughams, is better.

Draw the window outline in pencil on the front side of the canvas piece. Inside this outline, mark up a 1 in (2.5 cm) wide tabling, plus a half-inch (13 mm) tucking edge.

Cut a piece of window material to overlap the first outline drawn by half an inch, as shown by the dotted line. Lay the window down on the canvas and mark up the corners in bold pencil; turn over the work and mark the corners again on the inside

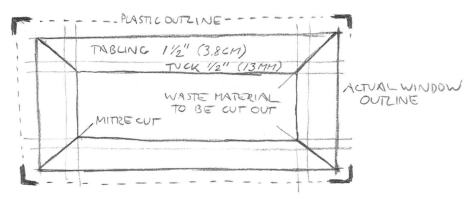

From the marked up side, cut out the hole for the window, making sure you are not cutting into the tabling allowances. Mitre cut at the four corners to make a slit back to the actual window outline.

Turn over the work and crease up the tabling flaps against the cloth. Place the plastic sheet on top of the hole that has been cut. It should fit into the corner marks made before. Draw a pencil outline all the way around the window, on the exposed side of the tabling flaps.

Sew a straight seam right around the window material, making sure the edge conforms with the outline drawn on the canvas. The seam should be as close to the edge of the plastic as possible.

When the seam has been taken right around, crease the remaining half-inch (13 mm) allowance towards the inside, fold it over and sew right around at the edge of the doubled canvas. This last tuck should follow the final outline of the window.

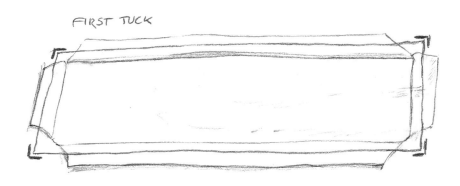

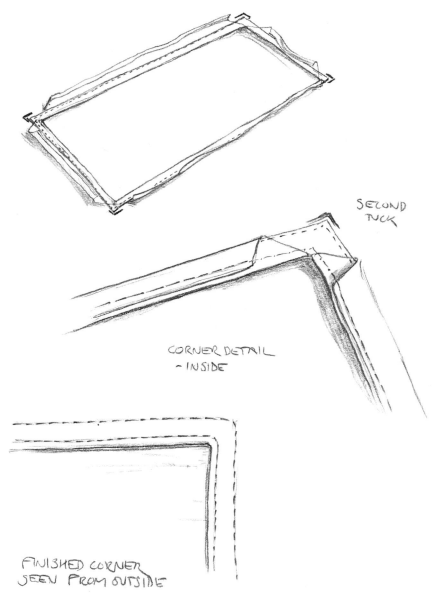

SECOND
TUCK

CORNER DETAIL
~ INSIDE

FINISHED CORNER
SEEN FROM OUTSIDE

With the window installed, if that was your choice, lay the front piece down on the roof piece as seen in the drawing. The half-inch mark-up on the front should coincide exactly with the 1 in mark-up at the front end of the roof piece. Fix the two cloths in place against one another, with staples if necessary, when putting in a straight machine seam along the two coinciding mark-up lines. Over the centre portion of the hood, a canvas strip can be sewn in to serve as hoop pocket later.

With the edges joined together, pull out the staples and crease the narrow edge down away from the first seam and the broad one down to encircle it. With the two parts of sprayhood flipped apart, put in a second seam close to the edge of the latest fold.

Now is a good time to drape the half-finished work over the hoops to see how well you are doing. There is no better model to make adjustments from than the actual structure.

Crease down the tabling marks on the triangular side pieces and put in tabling at top and bottom, sewing in a tension line at the junction.

Join the canvas to the sprayhood by the same turnover seam that joined the main parts of the hood. Take care that the 'right' side remains the same, that is, the side on which the turnover seams are taken, but opposite to the side into which the tablings are folded.

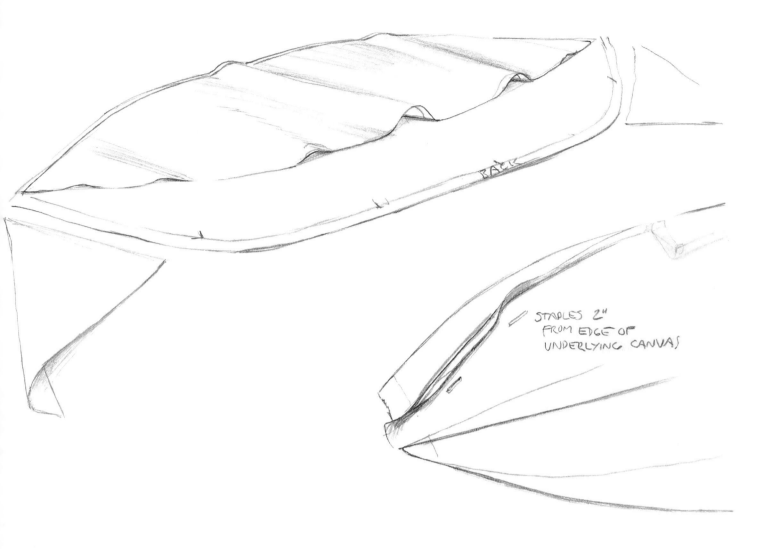

STAPLES 2"
FROM EDGE OF
UNDERLYING CANVAS

Between where the triangular pieces have been joined to the roof piece, fit a 4 in (10 cm) wide strip of canvas with half-inch (13 mm) borders folded over and creased. Make a turnover seam identical to the ones previously made, then turn the strip inside the sprayhood and sew it down with a straight seam along the edge. This is the pocket for the aft hoop.

Lastly, make sure the front hoop has a similar pocket and finish the lower end of the front piece with a tabling or roping to fit the turnbutton or grooved attachment.

BOTTOM

JOINS SPRAYHOOD

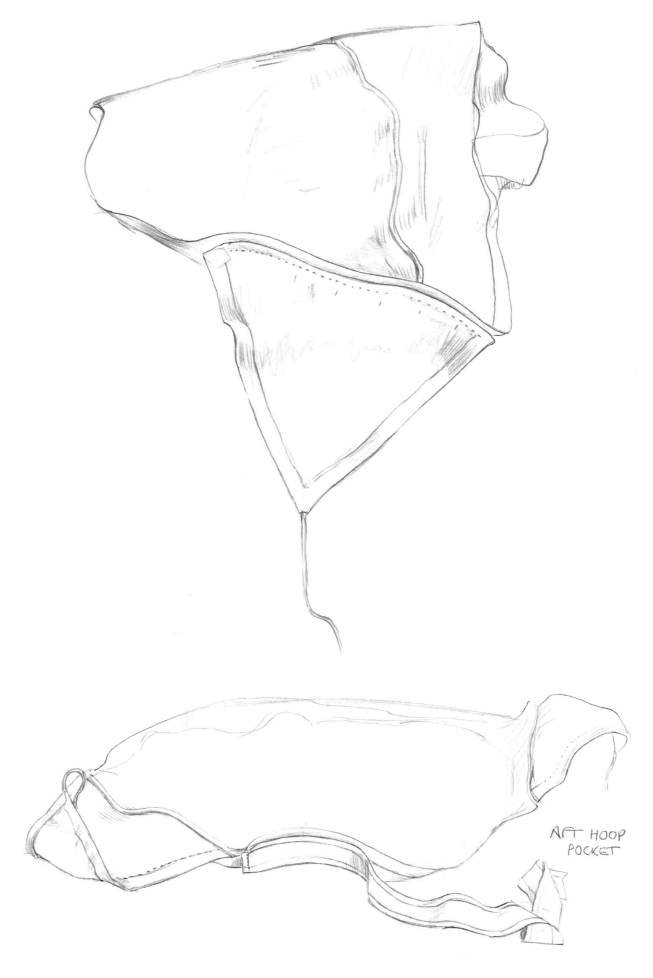

AFT HOOP
POCKET

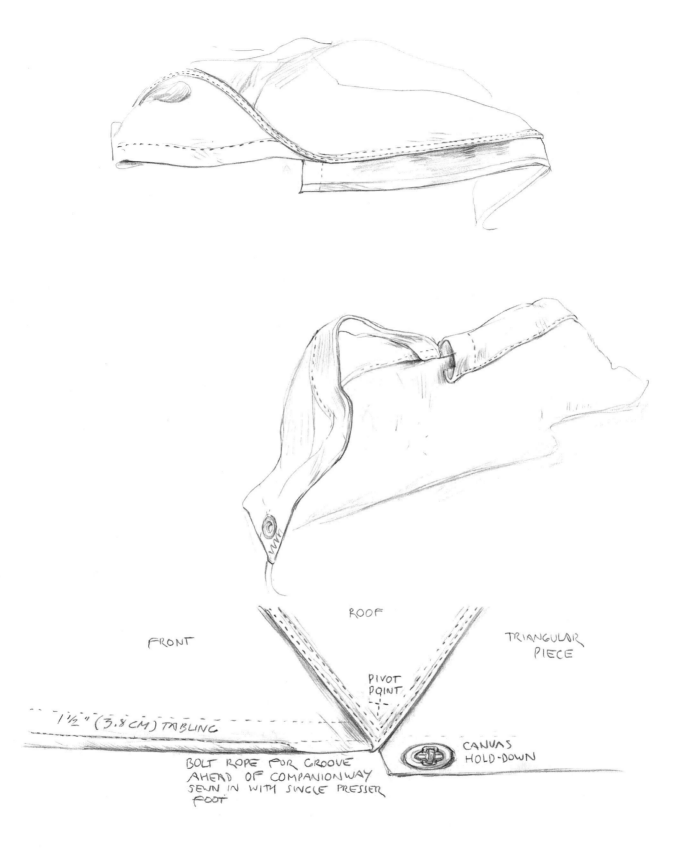

FRONT

ROOF

TRIANGULAR
PIECE

PIVOT
POINT

1½" (3.8 CM) TABLING

BOLT ROPE FOR GROOVE
AHEAD OF COMPANIONWAY
SEWN IN WITH SINGLE PRESSER
FOOT

CANVAS
HOLD-DOWN

At Ostia, my neighbour was Grant Dawson and his family from Palo Alto. Their sprayhood was an example of semi-permanent canvas cockpit protection, mounted on a double crossbar boom crutch and held aft by a conventional but heavy duty stainless steel hoop.

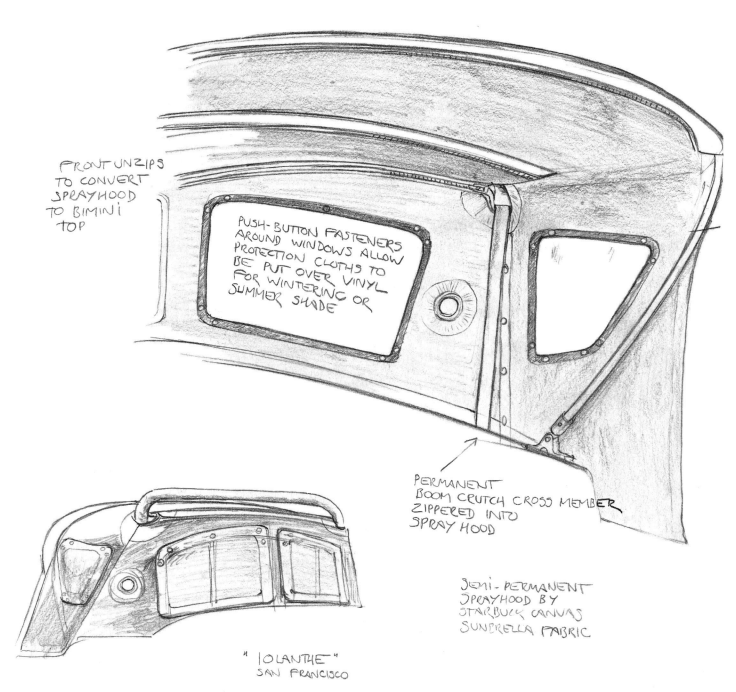

FRONT UNZIPS
TO CONVERT
SPRAYHOOD
TO BIMINI
TOP

PUSH-BUTTON FASTENERS
AROUND WINDOWS ALLOW
PROTECTION CLOTHS TO
BE PUT OVER VINYL
FOR WINTERING OR
SUMMER SHADE

PERMANENT
BOOM CRUTCH CROSS MEMBER
ZIPPERED INTO
SPRAY HOOD

SEMI-PERMANENT
SPRAYHOOD BY
STARBUCK CANVAS
SUNBRELLA FABRIC

" IOLANTHE "
SAN FRANCISCO

If a full cockpit cover is needed – in port during extreme weather conditions or a long-term stay – it is a fine way of extending the sheltered interior space. An extension can be made by adding a hoop aft of the sprayhood and cutting canvas to join up with the sprayhood. I did this while tied up at Ostia Antica and the result was as shown. The extension was joined to the sprayhood by means of a sleeve in the tabling forward, into which I fitted a drawstring which tightened over the aft sprayhood hoop.

In use, the greatest boon turned out to be zippered side and back flaps which could be rolled up on a coolish, windy day to allow the sun to enter the still sheltered space.

With a few other projects under your belt, this one should be fairly easy to tackle from scratch.

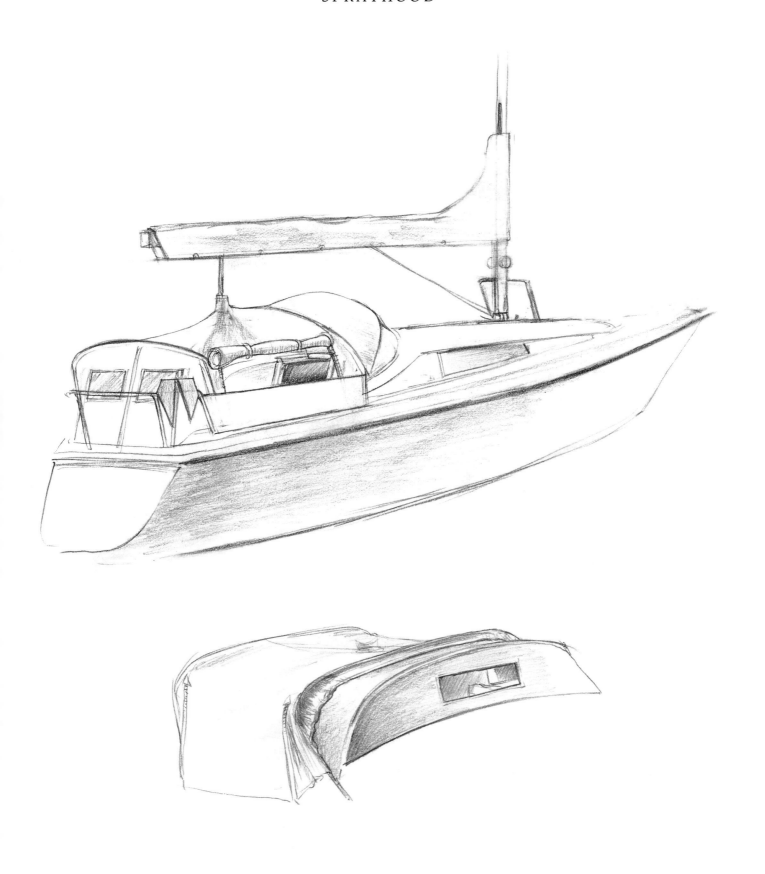

26

The bimini top

The bimini top has much in common with a sprayhood except for the absence of front and sides and a difference in purpose – it is purely for protection against the sun.

In constructing the frame, the bows should be made to collapse neatly, one on top of the other. It is often easier to have a bimini collapse aft rather than forward.

As with a sprayhood, make the bow pockets loose and generous in size and leave apertures for the four guys needed to hold the top in place.

The material is open to choice. Vinyl-coated fabrics are most often seen but acrylic would give more of a canvas look.

EXAMPLE OF CLOTH ARRANGEMENT
WHERE PANELS MEET AND A
POCKET IS CALLED FOR

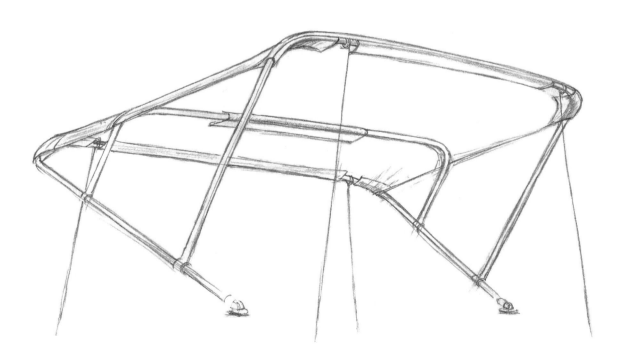

27
Awnings

In the Levant, an awning became a necessity. The first model, a blue Percale Matrimoniale or double bedsheet in time had to give way to a proper awning spread on a spar to give headroom and shade in the cockpit.

The material and colour were open to choice.

Lightweight nylon would have stowed easily, cotton would have looked and felt good, but to contain stretch at the spar-less forward and yet maintain the cotton look, I choose an acrylic weighing little more than 4 oz, and sold as 'tent fabric'.

I knew that white, or even off-white, creates glare and would partly defeat the main purpose of the awning, that of providing a shield from the sun, and therefore stuck to my first choice of the Percale, a deep royal blue verging on indigo. Another choice might have been a special cloth used in Italy which is white on top and blue underneath.

True to old shipboard practice, the cloths making up the awning should be started with the back or aftermost piece with each succeeding one forward lying on top at the flat felled seam overlap. If the cloths are laid fore and aft, starting out

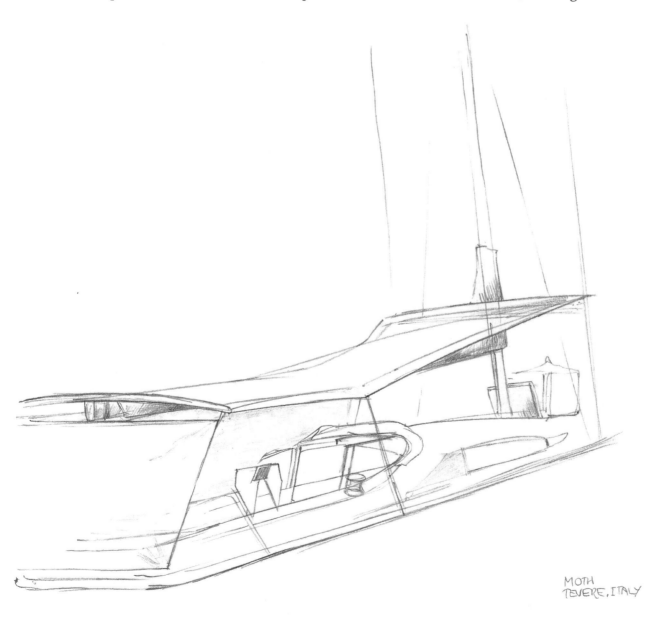

MOTH
TEVERE, ITALY

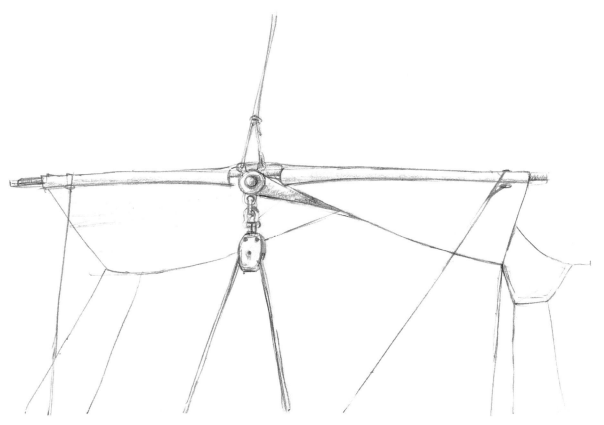

from the middle, succeeding cloths should be laid beneath. Making the cloth overlap this way serves the same purpose as in the similar laying of roof tiles, preventing moisture from being trapped and seeping through. Use a flat felled seam or, for a great deal of hand-seaming, a double flat seam.

My awning, like most others, was designed to lie on the main boom. Again, to follow loft practice, it should have had a chafing cloth, better known as the backbone, sewn in on the underside where the awning rests on the boom, but instead I simply overlapped two fore-and-aft running panels in the middle to create the same effect.

After determining the size of awning – in my case one that could be supported by a single aft spar with the front corners or earings strapped up to the shrouds – it is wise to deduct at least ten per cent before fixing the outline shape. To set beautifully and effectively, an awning must be small enough for the given space to stretch and set at proper tension.

In making a single-stick awning, make sure you allow for tablings of 1½ in width all around. Mark up the midpoint of the aft end – the example shown is slightly wider aft – and mark up a cut-out that allows a centre lashing for the spar to go in the aft sleeve.

Around the cut-out, mark a tucking allowance and cut mitres (as shown by the dotted lines) to the corners of the allowance.

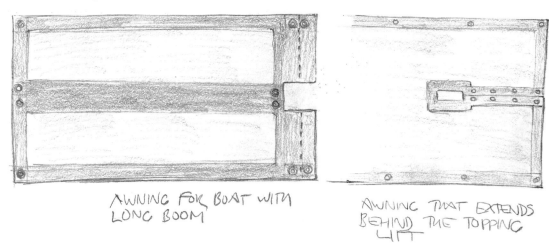

AWNING FOR BOAT WITH LONG BOOM

AWNING THAT EXTENDS BEHIND THE TOPPING LIFT

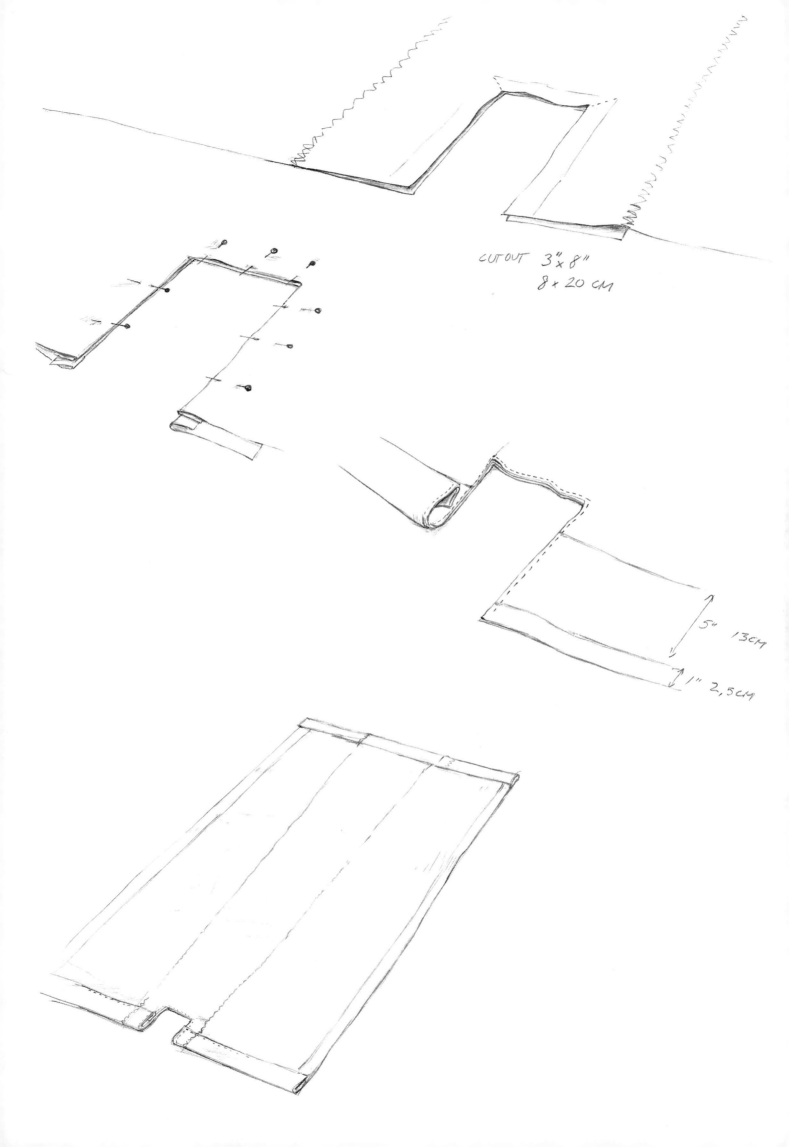

CUTOUT 3" x 8"
8 x 20 CM

5" 13CM

1" 2,5CM

Crease and tuck in both the centre cloth layers against one another as seen in the drawing and pin them in place. Take a straight seam near the edge.

In making the flat felled seams that join the panels, it is an advantage to pin the cloths together before taking the first straight seam, but if a very stout canvas is used this is not advisable.

Finally, consider adding corner patches as in a sail before you put in the tabling all around. Table the long sides first and take particular care to double stitch the sleeve that takes the stick and constitutes the aft tabling.

The mark-up recommendation for the sleeve, as shown in the drawing, must be adjusted to give the stick plenty of room. Eyelets can be put into the outside aft corners of the awning to help tensioning. At the forward corners they are of course obligatory.

There is much joy in first stretching the backbone tight and making fast a new awning, then balancing the tension on the corners on either side and using whatever lacings of additional strops you want.

For a perfect fit, the awning must be made according to the type and size of your boat, the final cut and set showing off your canvas-working ability.

For a boat with an overall length of over 20 ft, you will probably want to fit a forward supporting spar as well as the aft one.

" CHRISMARY II "

VILLE FRANCHE-
JUR-MER

As the awning size increases, additional batten pockets across the awning to divide it into equal portions, will make it more stable.

The material for the end pieces and battens can be wood – my own is Polish beech – aluminium tubing or fibreglass tent poles. Bamboo can also be used.

An alternative, or additional, way of controlling and shaping the awning is to fit lifts to the upper side as shown in the sketch of *Chrismary*.

If the awning is to be set high above the main boom, a common practice in the 60 to 80 ft range sailing boats is to use a rope or webbing backbone. Better still is a ridge pole running fore and aft as a substitute for the boom.

Whatever the exact style, beginning with a simple top piece with the option of adding side curtains allows easy setting and adjustment. With such a panelled awning, two extra curtains, one for the back and one for the side, will be sufficient cover if they are shifted around depending on the slant of the sun or direction of the wind.

Where an awning meets side curtains, eyelet lacing holes must be provide at regular intervals on either side. The lace-up line is then hitched to an eyelet halfway along, minimising the length of line that has to be rove through when lacing the two pieces together.

Certain rules serve well in the making of an awning. To start with, a well defined 1½ in tabling with a one and a quarter inch tuck underneath will provide a firm outline with solid anchorage for eyelets and lacing.

To add strength, sew a luff rope along the creased endge of the tuck. Even a small diameter line, ³⁄₁₆ in (4.8 mm) in diameter, will do fine service. Polypropylene line is a good choice, being cheap, unlikely to shrink and fairly strong.

For heavy-duty work, a rope can be sewn to the underneath side of the finished tabling, in the same manner as when fitting a luff rope. Put in a roping stitch all around and join the ends with a short splice before that too is roped on.

To contain stretch at the corners or earings, clew patches should be sewn in with the tabling. Use the same material as in the awning, with the warp and weft lined up to match. Be liberal with the size of the reinforcements and tuck under and sew in the slanted side.

All reinforcements, clew patches and the turn of the tabling should be on the lower side of the awning.

Where a 'shark's jaw' has to be made to accommodate the topping lift or a shroud, sew on a piece matching the cut-off with the edges tucked underneath to meet a tuck in the awning cut-out. Thus, the raw edge of the cut is sewn in and the edge strengthened to take eyelet lacing or a Delrin zipper.

The spacing of eyelet tie-downs around an awning will depend on its size, weight and use. On the *Moth*, the sun awning has eyelets at only the corners and a pair at the halfway mark to allow for tie-down and shape control.

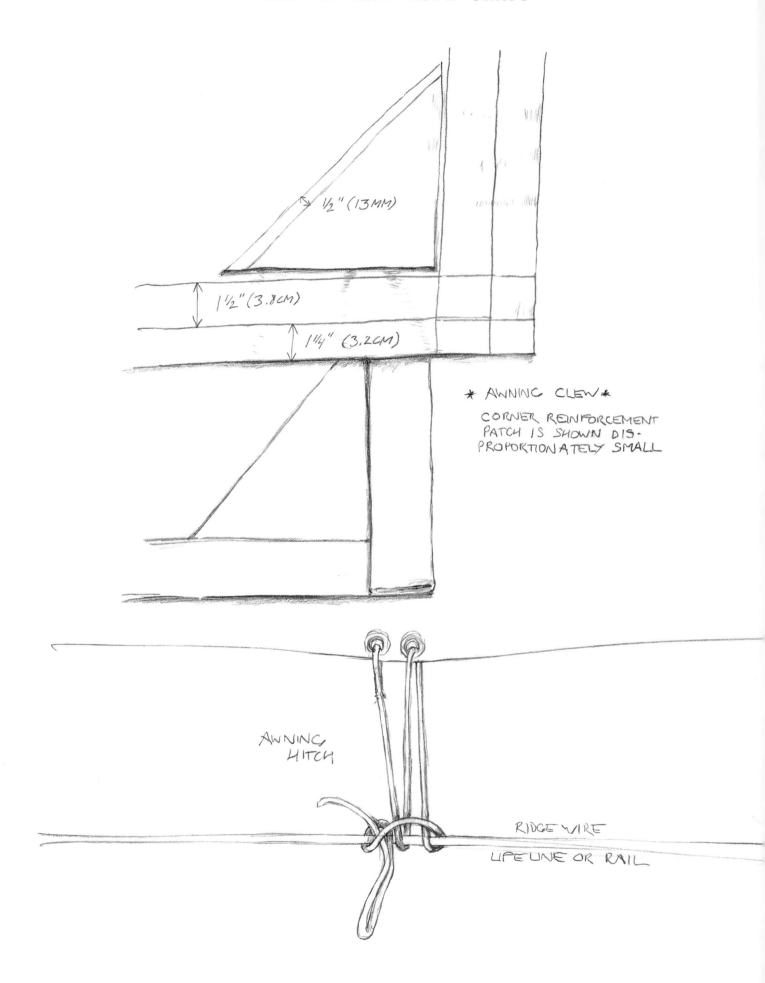

½" (13MM)

1½" (3.8CM)

1¼" (3.2CM)

* AWNING CLEW *

CORNER REINFORCEMENT
PATCH IS SHOWN DIS-
PROPORTIONATELY SMALL

AWNING
HITCH

RIDGE WIRE

LIFELINE OR RAIL

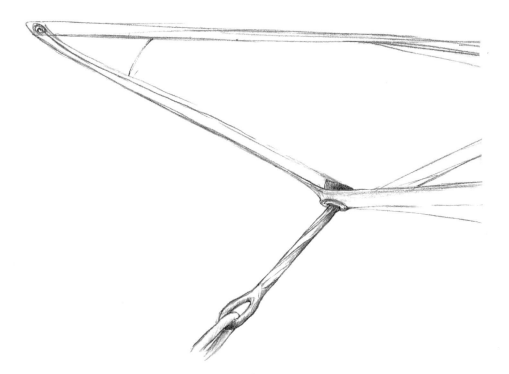

Larger size awnings will require lacing to ridge wires, in practice consisting of the life lines or rail of the boat. Most often, a running lacing will be used to hold down the edge or side curtains of the awning, as shown in the *Chrismary* sketch.

It is much better to fit eyelets in pairs, especially at either end of the awnings backbone, so a strop can be spliced in and the points hauled tight with a decent purchase. If secured with an awning hitch, as shown, this arrangement gives a fine set and a quick release that does not jam.

In blustery conditions, you may want some give in the tie-downs. Lorry tarpaulin strops can be handier for such use than the customary shock-cord.

28
The fixed canvas top

In Menton I came across a Briton who had tired of the noonday sun and fitted a permanent canvas top in the style once seen on the bridge of ships.

In a consistently hot climate there is much to be said for this arrangement, especially if the support tubing is arranged to fit into existing stanchion bases.

Acrylic canvas is a good material to use and the sleeves for the tubing can be made from canvas strips that are doubled and have the raw edges sewn in.

If the strip is then fitted with a double row of eyelets and sewn in along the middle, a running lace-up can be made along the tubing for a firm and smart set.

At edges, as when lacing to a rail, a single piece of webbing can be sewn on to hold eyelets, as shown in the second drawing.

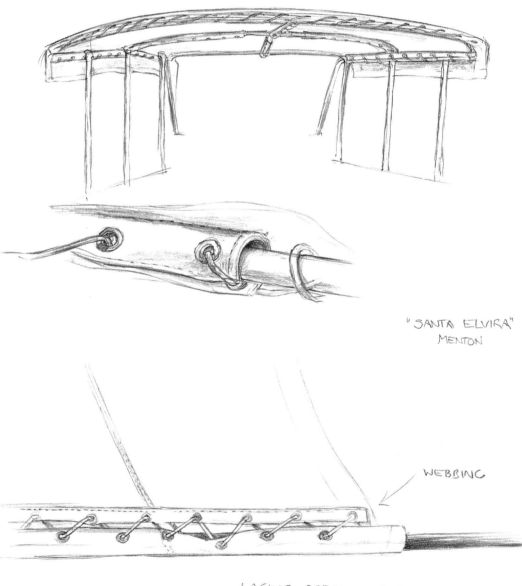

"SANTA ELVIRA"
MENTON

WEBBING

LACING ARRANGEMENT
AROUND A RAIL

29

Boat covers

For in-the-water storage, a full cover keeps everything topside in mint condition. Acrylic is again an obvious choice in material, seeing that it 'breathes' better than a totally waterproof or vinyl-coated material. A good fit is important to prevent puddles forming and leaking through, or making loose flaps that can be caught by the wind.

There should be through ventilation fore-and-aft, if necessary provided by fitting scoops as shown in the drawing. The scoop has plenty of extra material to set properly over a tabled aperture in the cover.

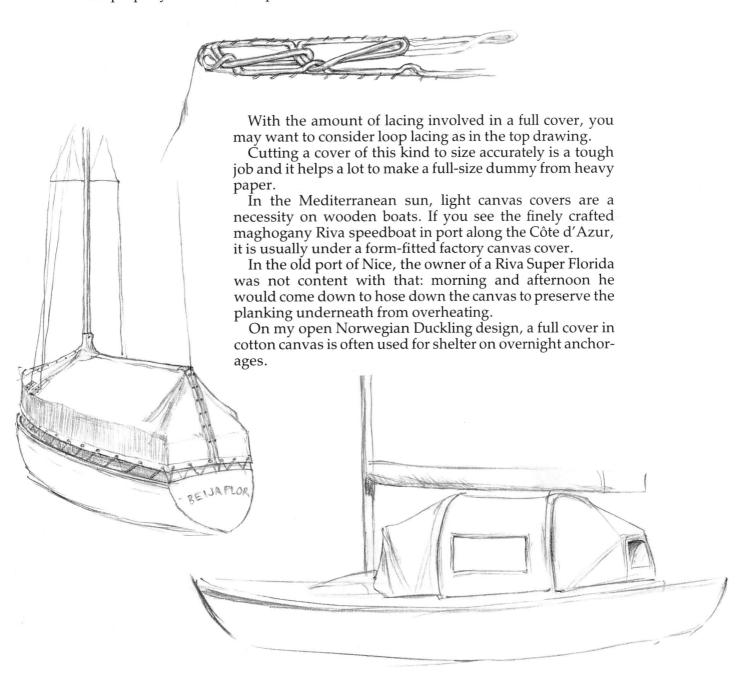

With the amount of lacing involved in a full cover, you may want to consider loop lacing as in the top drawing.

Cutting a cover of this kind to size accurately is a tough job and it helps a lot to make a full-size dummy from heavy paper.

In the Mediterranean sun, light canvas covers are a necessity on wooden boats. If you see the finely crafted maghogany Riva speedboat in port along the Côte d'Azur, it is usually under a form-fitted factory canvas cover.

In the old port of Nice, the owner of a Riva Super Florida was not content with that: morning and afternoon he would come down to hose down the canvas to preserve the planking underneath from overheating.

On my open Norwegian Duckling design, a full cover in cotton canvas is often used for shelter on overnight anchorages.

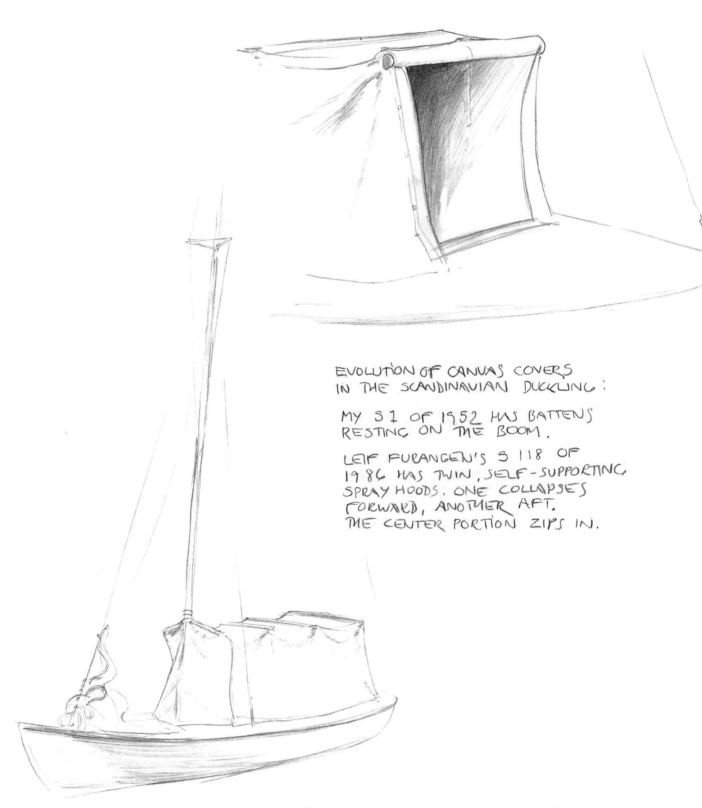

EVOLUTION OF CANVAS COVERS
IN THE SCANDINAVIAN DUCKLING:

MY S1 OF 1952 HAS BATTENS
RESTING ON THE BOOM.

LEIF FURANGEN'S S 118 OF
1986 HAS TWIN, SELF-SUPPORTING
SPRAY HOODS. ONE COLLAPSES
FORWARD, ANOTHER AFT.
THE CENTER PORTION ZIPS IN.

There are delrin zippers at all four corners so the sides and back flap can be raised at will.

Thanks to the battens sewn in at the top and resting on the boom, there is plenty of room inside and full standing headroom. Rain makes the canvas swell up and become waterproof.

Sailing with such a contrivance stowed away, you have all the advantages of an open boat by day and fine weather. Coming to an anchorage, wind or rain will not

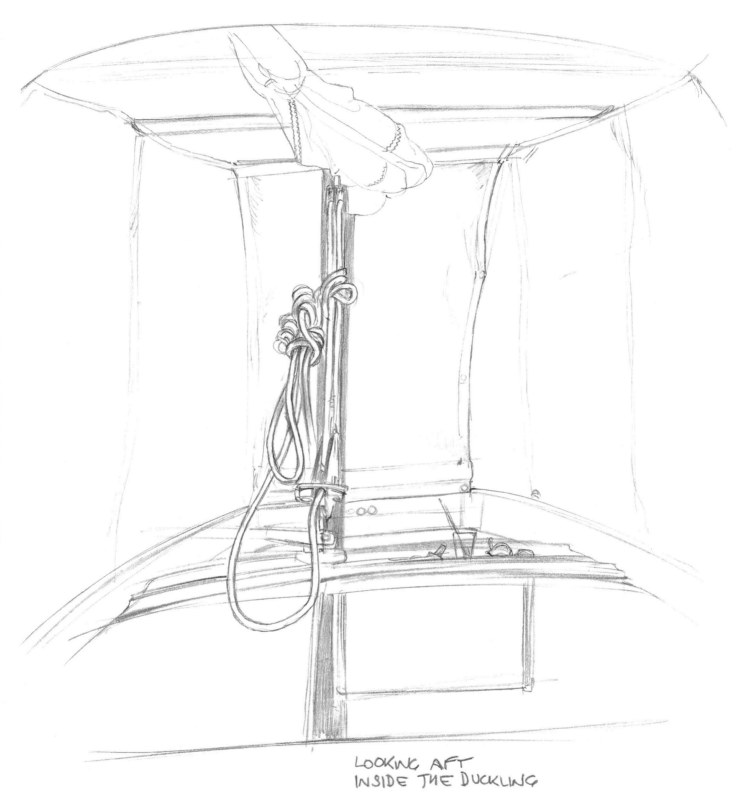

LOOKING AFT
INSIDE THE DUCKLING

bother you much once the cover rests on the boom and the wide flaps have been let down. With the flaps zippered at the corners aft and halfway forward, a 'curtain' can be rolled up against the side away from the wind or facing the sun. With all the side curtains rolled up you have a fine flat sun screen over your head.

As night draws near, you develop a fine feeling for when the dew is about to fall and you learn never to delay setting up the cover beyond that point.

On cold nights, a single oil lamp will keep the interior snug and dry as you tuck yourself in with an Arthur Ransome feeling in your gut.

30
The wind scoop

In the heat of July with runaway forest fires sweeping the coastal mountains around Dubrovnik, I made a wind scoop.

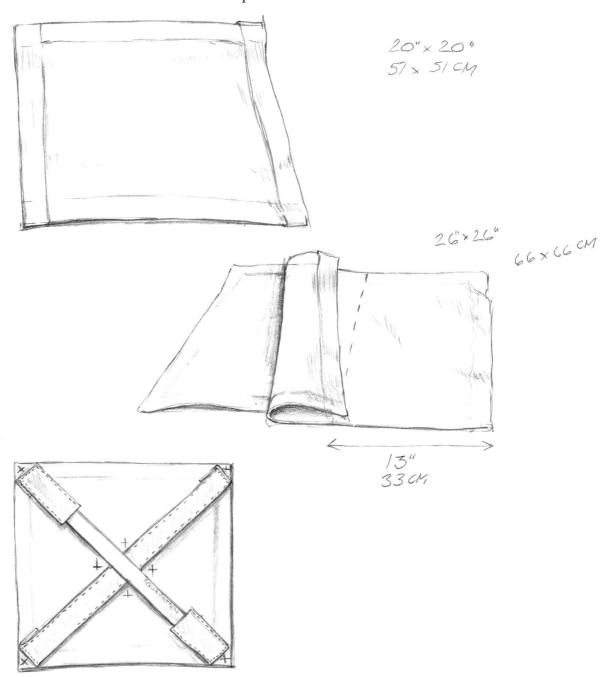

20" x 20"
51 x 51 CM

26" x 26"
66 x 66 CM

13"
33 CM

After trying some makeshift arrangements with the hammock strung up the mast and funnelled down the forward hatch, it was obvious that the scattered puffs that did move over the water needed to be caught by a radar reflector-style scoop, facing all directions.

To make one, locate two spare battens and some material – anything that is light and stable and easy to sew. The size will depend on the size of your hatch and the measurements given with the drawings are for a hatch of 20 in × 20 in (50 × 50 cm) and without tabling allowance.

Put in the customary one and half an inch (3.8 cm) tabling with half an inch (13 mm) tuck under all around.

On the top piece, sew down webbing or selvedged Dacron tape to make batten pockets. Cut the battens to size. Make grommet holes as indicated by the tiny crosses near the centre and at the end of the batten projection.

Sew together the two other pieces (shown on top of one another in the drawing) with two or three straight seams at 13 in or halfway from the ends.

Put small grommets in all corners and at the upper inside junction. This gives you a small but quite efficient unit for a flush, deck-mounted hatch. To elevate the entry a bit and get a free wind flow going, add the skirt shown in the drawing. A kite-stick arrangement – two crossed and lashed sticks – is added at the foot of the scoop proper to give a fixed spread to it. The ends are tapered to fit snugly into the grommet holes. Put a drawstring around the hatch coaming.

July in Yugoslavia will become quite bearable. Even so, a 12-volt fan – such as I purchased later in Antibes – is a welcome complement when the temperature goes beyond 30°C (90°F).

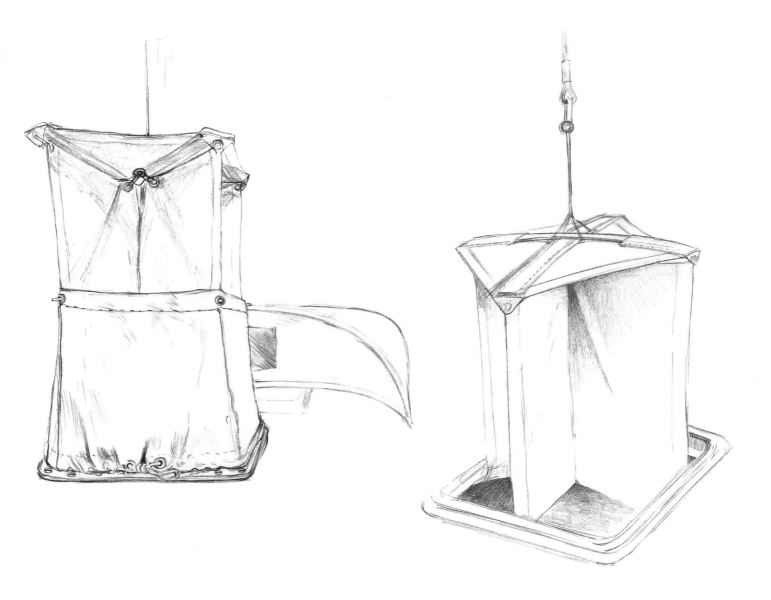

31

A note on sailmaking

Some of the best sailmakers I have known were largely self-taught. In stark contrast stood Herr Andersson, a superb hand seaming man taught in a loft since childhood but never having had any interest in sailing.

There is a great joy in setting sails of your own making but it is an art that falls a bit outside general canvas work. Yet, a few words will not be amiss, in particular to provide a framework for doing sail repairs.

To make a sail, you first produce a full-size image of it, preferably on a level floor.

To lay down the measurements, use a sail plan obtained from the designer or taken from the spar measurements or foretriangle.

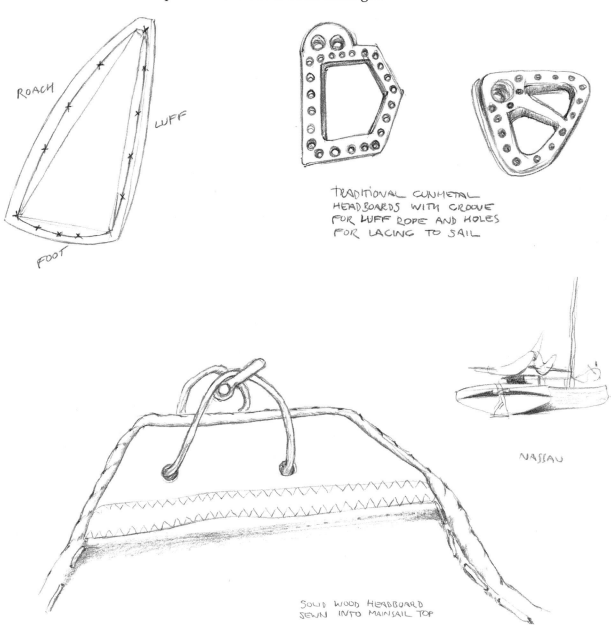

ROACH

LUFF

FOOT

TRADITIONAL GUNMETAL HEADBOARDS WITH GROOVE FOR LUFF ROPE AND HOLES FOR LACING TO SAIL

NASSAU

SOLID WOOD HEADBOARD SEWN INTO MAINSAIL TOP

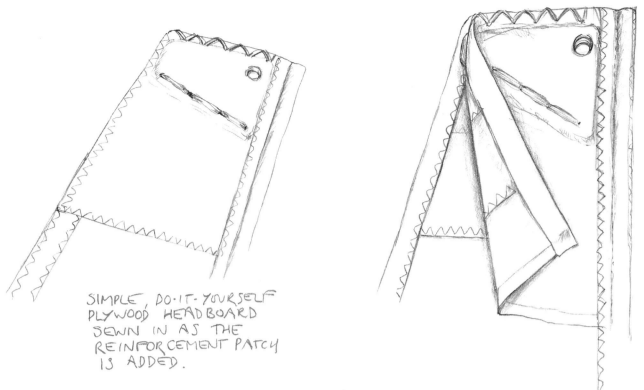

Measure up luff, foot and leech, noting that the headboard will need extra width at the top end of the sail. Mark the corners of the sail with awls stuck into the floor and draw straight chalk lines in between.

Make chalk marks for the amount of roach and fullness in luff and foot. Lay a flexible batten along these marks, bending it to a fair curve so a line can be drawn along it as a guide for cutting.

This makes the traditional type of sail image from which you can work.

To realise your image, pass a bolt of sail cloth back and forth, starting at the tack seam. Cut the cloth so that each panel overlaps the sail image by 2 in. The tack seam strikes the leech at right angles to prevent stretch on the bias of the material. Usually, each succeeding panel overlaps by 1 in and there is usually a faint blue marker line in Dacron at the edge of the Dacron cloths which then run together as one.

Mark the amount of broadseaming you want to put in the seams, that is, the overlap of the panels to create fullness in the sail. In a mainsail, as a rough guide, you would want broadseaming forward of the shadow marked in the drawing, at least in the tack seam and the two above it.

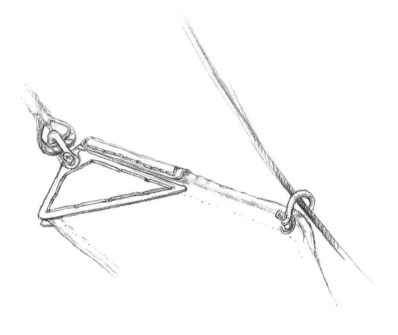

SPONGE FISHING BOAT
"AHESTE"

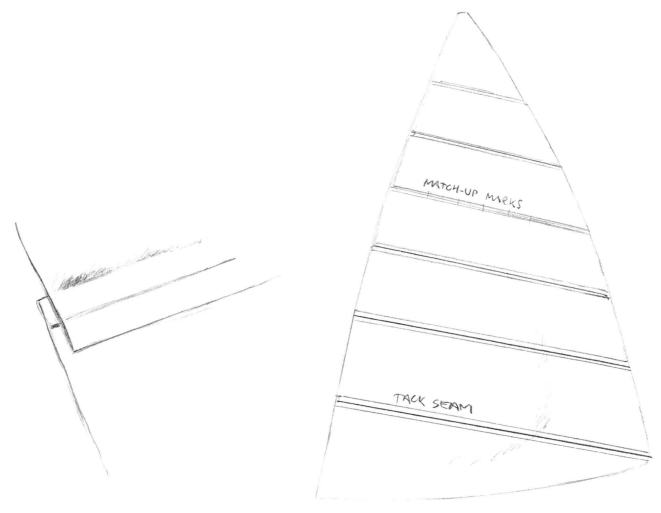

The shape in the sail is the product of fullness in the outline of the cut sail, combined with broadseaming. Stretch used to be another great factor to be considered when cutting cotton and flax sails but now this problem has been brought down to a mere fraction of what it used to be.

When all the panels have been joined, lay down the 'raw' sail on the floor plan again. With awls again holding critical points, draw the definitive sail outline on the actual sail. Flexible battens may again be used.

The choice is now between a turned over tabling edge or an independent, sewn on sail tape. A simple, turned over tabling means marking lines at 1½ in (3.6 cm) and 2 in (5 cm) outside the finished sail outline. On the luff and foot this should be changed to lines at 1½ in (3.8 cm) and 3 in (7.6 cm) outside the planned sail.

In the first instance, the outside edge is creased at the outside line, to bring a double fold up against the inner guideline as shown in the drawing.

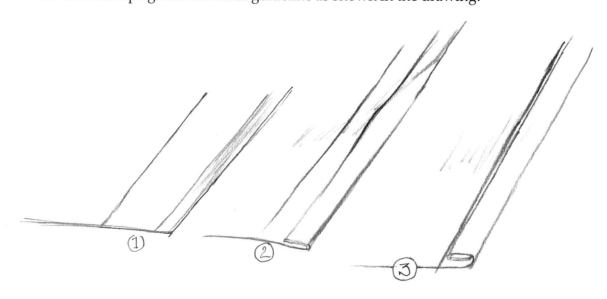

In the second case, simply crease hard on the lines and fold twice as above. In both cases, finish with a zig-zag seam on the edge of the inner, exposed edge of the fold.

When drawing up the leech, draw straight lines between the batten pockets to avoid flutter from excess material outside the straight lines. A hard weather cruising main can even be hollowed out on the leech and battens discarded altogether.

The drawback of a turned over tabling is that it can pinch up where the edge of the sail is curved or comes to the edge on a bias, such as at the luff. To prevent this, and yet avoid having to use a sail tape, cut a strip from outside the outline of the sail, leaving a half-inch wide sewing allowance outside the outline marked. Crease half-inch (13 mm) wide tucks on the edge of the makeshift tape you have cut out and sew down on the sail after its edge has been creased also.

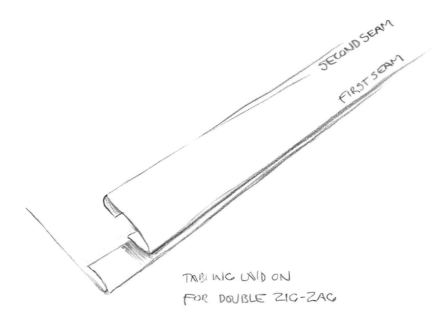

If you have a sail tape compatible with the cloth laid out, crease it down along the middle and sew it on flat along one outside edge, the middle crease mark coinciding with the outline of the sail. Fold over and take the second zig-zag to fix the tape. If you want a luff rope sewn in, insert it before taking the second seam and finish with a third, single presser foot straight seam against the rope.

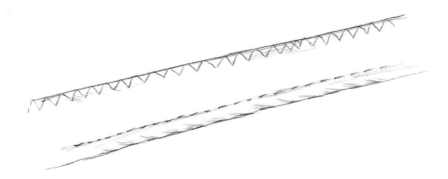

The sail must be fixed to the luff at top and bottom with hand stitching. To fix the tension along the length of the luff, it is customary to make stops at regular

ALL HALYARDS
FASTENED WITH
BOWLINES

THE 5¼ OZ MAXIMUM HEADSAIL IS
SNAP SHACKLED TO A FOOT-LONG
WIRE STROP IN THE BOW

A LEATHER STRIP ON THE FOOT
GUARDS AGAINST CHAFE WHERE
THE SAIL PASSES OVER THE PULPIT

intervals, particularly if a wire luff is involved. If wire is used, it is common to
strike eyelets at top and bottom of the luff next to a sleeve provided for the wire
which in turn has eyes at either end. The tautness of the sail luff can then be
adjusted with the lashings.

For cruising, a polypropylene rope luff is much better to handle.

32

Cruising sails

When the mainsail on the *Moth* suddenly blew out under the stormy shore of Tinos in the Cyclades, I decided to make a main that had some built-in safety and anti-chafe features.

I changed nothing in the basic design of the sail, nor in cloth weight, and the features could be incorporated into any sail with enough value to need preventive maintenance. First, I locked up the aft end of the sail panel seams with a square patch to prevent them coming apart as a result of chafe on the leech tabling. The tabling itself was given a third seam for added strength.

To keep the spreaders from poking through the sail I put patches on either side

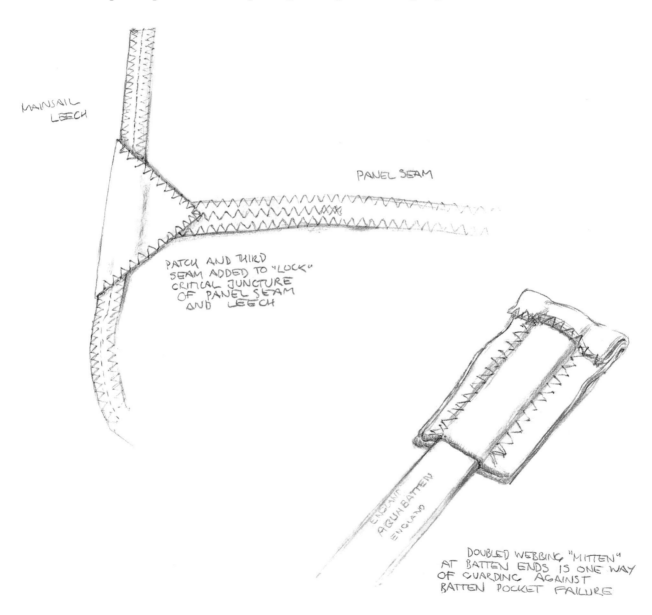

MAINSAIL LEECH

PANEL SEAM

PATCH AND THIRD SEAM ADDED TO "LOCK" CRITICAL JUNCTURE OF PANEL SEAM AND LEECH

ENGLAND AQUABATTEN ENGLAND

DOUBLED WEBBING "MITTEN" AT BATTEN ENDS IS ONE WAY OF GUARDING AGAINST BATTEN POCKET FAILURE

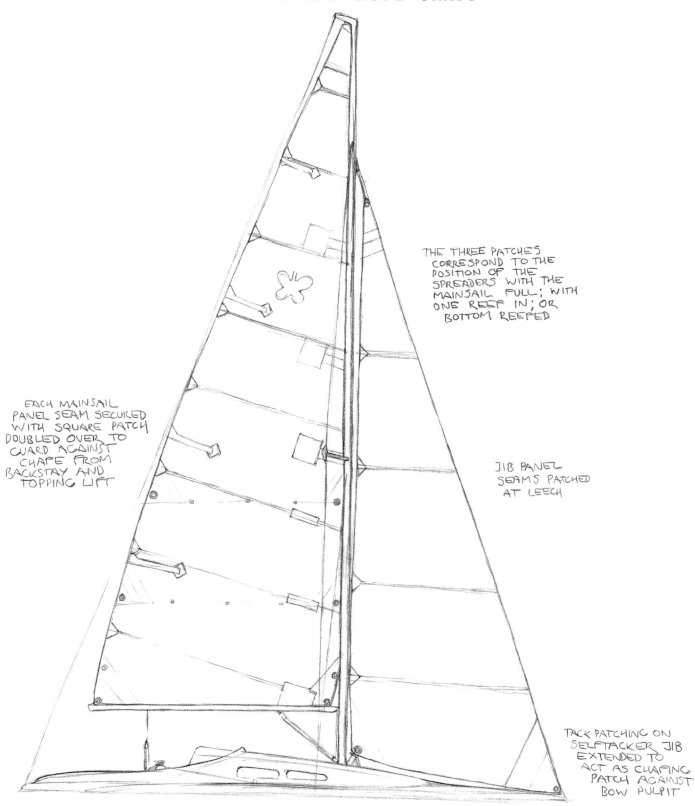

THE THREE PATCHES
CORRESPOND TO THE
POSITION OF THE
SPREADERS WITH THE
MAINSAIL FULL; WITH
ONE REEF IN; OR
BOTTOM REEFED

EACH MAINSAIL
PANEL SEAM SECURED
WITH SQUARE PATCH
DOUBLED OVER TO
GUARD AGAINST
CHAFE FROM
BACKSTAY AND
TOPPING LIFT

JIB PANEL
SEAMS PATCHED
AT LEECH

TACK PATCHING ON
SELFTACKER JIB
EXTENDED TO
ACT AS CHAFING
PATCH AGAINST
BOW PULPIT

"MOTH" WORKING SAILS

THE SPREADERS ARE
ANGLED BACK 28° SO THERE
IS A PATCH TO GUARD
AGAINST THE SPREADER
TIP AND SOME MORE
TO PROTECT THE SEAMS
FROM ABRASION AGAINST
THE SHROUDS.

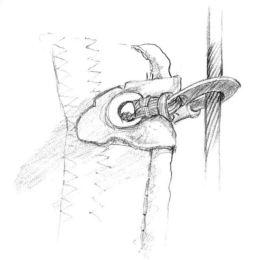

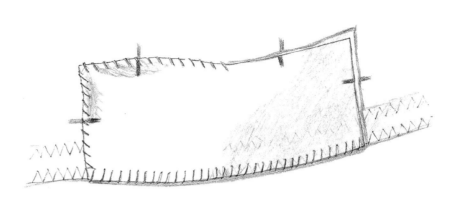

PISTON HANK EYELET
BEDDED IN LEATHER

and in places where the spreaders would end up with the sail reefed. To keep the panel seams from chafing open at the inboard end, where they came in contact with the lower portion of the shrouds, I sewed sail tape over the seams. Another chafe patch on the foot round of the sail kept it from chafing through when caught between the main boom and the shrouds.

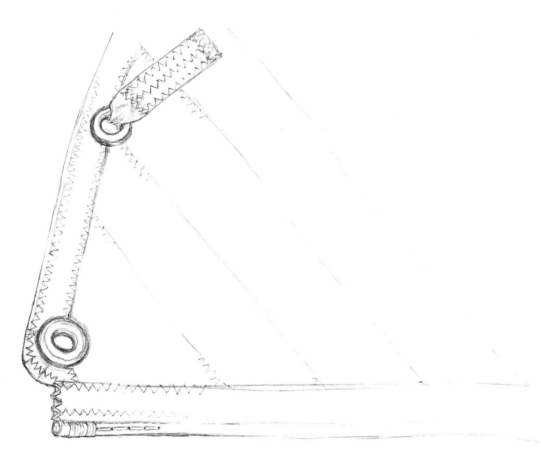

I did the chafe patching only after a week of using the sail on the boat. That way, it was possible to see and mark up exactly where the patches should be situated.

To finish, I put some heavy webbing into the reef cringles to further spread the load from them over the sail.

To make a cruising headsail to match, I added only leech patches and an extra large patch at the tack to keep the sail from chafing through against the pulpit.

Already, both sails have more mileage than the bought ones, yet are ageing more gracefully.

33

Rope

In nautical use, rope is closely allied to canvas work. The traditional hemp, sisal, coir, and Manila cordage was made from the natural fibres of the hemp plant, the agave, the coconut and the Philippine banana respectively.

Foremost came Bologna hemp, which in its untarred variety was the easiest cordage to handle. Hemp fibres separated from the rope were useful as yarn for handseaming or whipping.

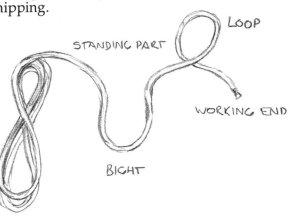

STANDING PART

LOOP

WORKING END

BICHT

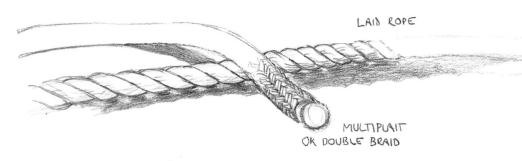

LAID ROPE

MULTIPLAIT
OR DOUBLE BRAID

THREE-STRAND

Most of the natural fibre rope was laid up in three stages. First the yarns were twisted clockwise, then the bunch of yarns which were to form a strand were twisted together anti-clockwise. Finally, these strands were twisted together clockwise to form 'right-handed' rope, usually of three strands.

If four strands were used, a core or 'heart' line was usually put in the middle to make a rounded rope.

Such rope was invariably measured in its inch circumference rather than, as is common now, in its metric diameter. And so, the 1 in rope has become the 8 mm, the 1½ in the 12 mm, and so forth.

But the greatest change has been to synthetic fibres derived from raw oil and coal. Beginning with nylon, which has a strength perhaps three times that of Manila rope, manufactured fibres like Dacron and polypropylene have taken over. Ropes made from them are stronger and, most importantly, do not rot.

Nevertheless, chafe is a hazard and polypropylene rope in particular deteriorates if hot and exposed. In canvas work and sailmaking it is best sewn in as a boltrope and protected by the canvas pocket it lies in.

Nylon sees most use in mooring lines and towlines because of its elasticity; Dacron stretches little and therefore serves well in sheets, halyards and in such things as hammock slings.

In nylon and polypropylene, the three-strand is still the most common lay while polyester (Dacron) is mostly plaited or braided with an inner and outer part.

For canvas work, three-strand laid rope with its perfectly balanced parts and clearly defined contlines is still the best lay, whether you are taking a strand out of it to manufacture a three-strand, circular rope grommet, or simply rope stitching it to the outline of a sail or awning.

Treat all cordage well, rinsing its salt out along with the sails and other canvas and storing it in a dry place, if possible out of the sun. Let it lie in loose horizontal coils or, when made up into a coil, with the twist it wants to take on as shown here with a length of Dacron.

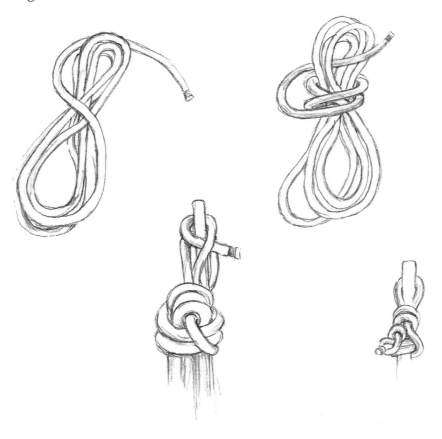

There is every reason to learn to finish properly the ends of a rope to prevent the sad sight of what is variously known as 'fag end', 'dead men', 'Irish pennant', and 'cow's tail'.

Make a sewn whipping: it is the most secure and has the added advantage that two ends can be securely hitched together to go aloft through a sheave.

The illustration shows a sewn whipping made with a doubled fathom of twine in three-strand and braided line.

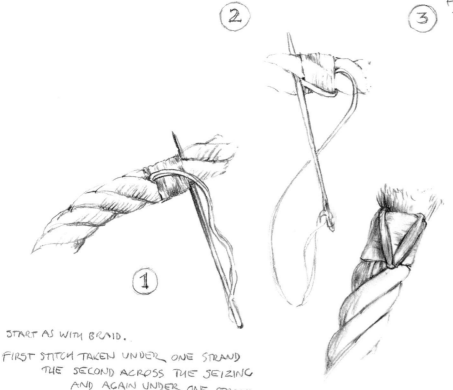

ROTATE THE WORK TOWARDS YOU AND STITCH BACK TO WHERE THE FIRST STITCH EMERGED, UNDER ONE STRAND:

②

③ CONTINUE IN THE SAME ZIG-ZAG FASHION FOR ANOTHER FOUR STITCHES TO COMPLETE THE WHIPPING.

FOR A SLIGHTLY SIMPLER WHIPPING, TAKE THE FRAPPING TURNS ONLY ALONG THE GROOVES BETWEEN STRANDS = THE CONTLINES, OMITTING THE ZIG-ZAG EFFECT

EITHER WAY HEAVE HOME THE FRAPPING TURNS WITH GUSTO AND BURY THE TWINE BEFORE CUTTING

①

START AS WITH BRAID.

FIRST STITCH TAKEN UNDER ONE STRAND THE SECOND ACROSS THE SEIZING AND AGAIN UNDER ONE STRAND

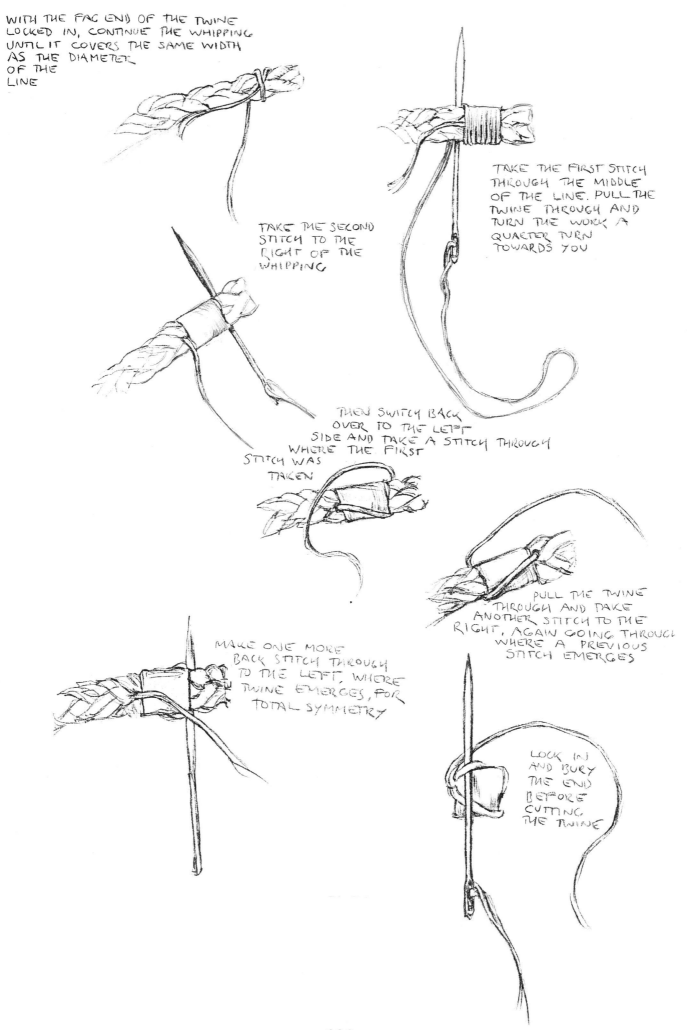

WITH THE FAG END OF THE TWINE
LOCKED IN, CONTINUE THE WHIPPING
UNTIL IT COVERS THE SAME WIDTH
AS THE DIAMETER
OF THE
LINE

TAKE THE FIRST STITCH
THROUGH THE MIDDLE
OF THE LINE. PULL THE
TWINE THROUGH AND
TURN THE WORK A
QUARTER TURN
TOWARDS YOU

TAKE THE SECOND
STITCH TO THE
RIGHT OF THE
WHIPPING

THEN SWITCH BACK
OVER TO THE LEFT
SIDE AND TAKE A STITCH THROUGH
WHERE THE FIRST
STITCH WAS
TAKEN

PULL THE TWINE
THROUGH AND TAKE
ANOTHER STITCH TO THE
RIGHT, AGAIN GOING THROUGH
WHERE A PREVIOUS
STITCH EMERGES

MAKE ONE MORE
BACK STITCH THROUGH
TO THE LEFT, WHERE
TWINE EMERGES, FOR
TOTAL SYMMETRY

LOCK IN
AND BURY
THE END
BEFORE
CUTTING
THE TWINE

133

34
Knots

The accomplished canvas worker should know his knots. There is no greater pleasure after making a piece of canvas than setting it up to advantage with properly knotted and tautened cordage.

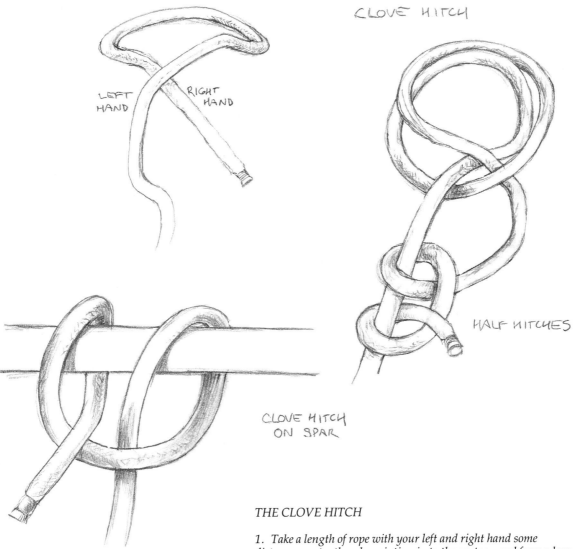

CLOVE HITCH

LEFT HAND   RIGHT HAND

HALF HITCHES

CLOVE HITCH ON SPAR

THE CLOVE HITCH

1. Take a length of rope with your left and right hand some distance apart – thumbs pointing in to the centre – and form a loop by quickly moving your right hand in towards and slightly below your left hand.

2. Drop your left hand to clasp the crossover point as your right hand slides out along the rope to the right, takes a hold on the rope some distance out, and is brought back quickly to the left and twisted clockwise to form another loop on top of the first one. Drop on bollard or cleat and tighten up.

I have served no apprenticeship in knots except that of living on or near the sea. You had to learn your knots as the need for them arose.

With the task of tying up boats traditionally falling to the youngest hand, you quickly had to master the double half hitch and clove hitch. For safety, the clove hitch would always get the benefit of another double half hitch on the standing part.

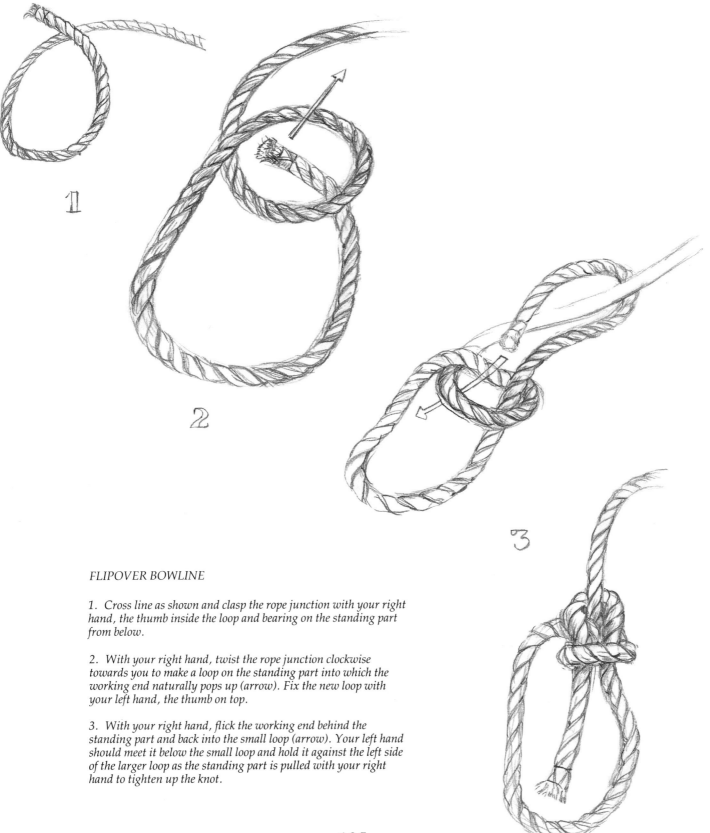

FLIPOVER BOWLINE

1. Cross line as shown and clasp the rope junction with your right hand, the thumb inside the loop and bearing on the standing part from below.

2. With your right hand, twist the rope junction clockwise towards you to make a loop on the standing part into which the working end naturally pops up (arrow). Fix the new loop with your left hand, the thumb on top.

3. With your right hand, flick the working end behind the standing part and back into the small loop (arrow). Your left hand should meet it below the small loop and hold it against the left side of the larger loop as the standing part is pulled with your right hand to tighten up the knot.

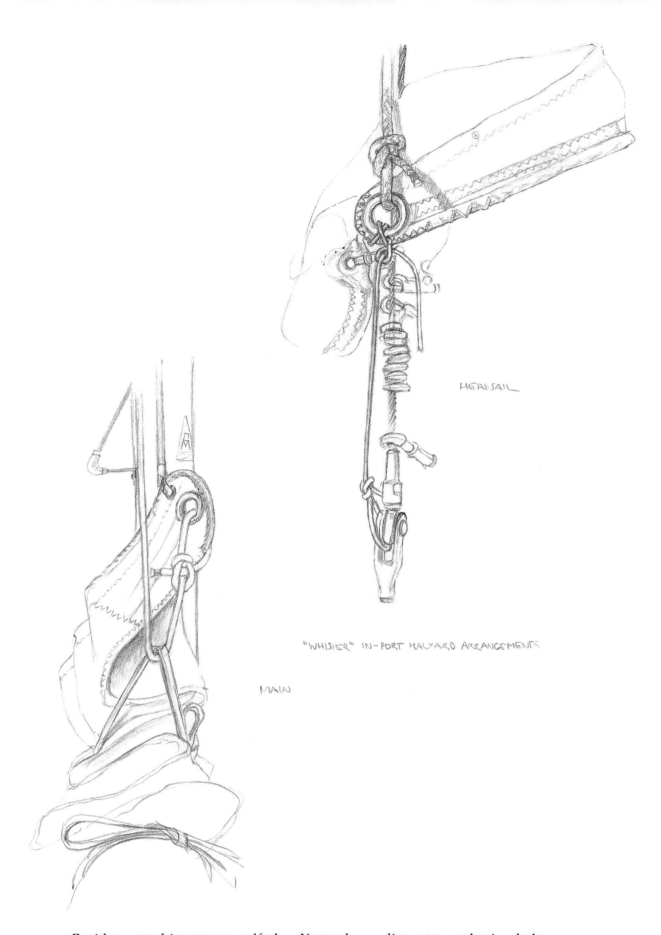

HEADSAIL

"WHISPER" IN-PORT HALYARD ARRANGEMENTS

MAIN

Besides, watching my grandfather Konrad mending nets and tying belts, you learnt the square knot and macramé. He also taught me and my cousins the superbly useful bowline, not by the cumbersome rabbit-in-the-hole style but by the swift and elegant flip-over method. To practise it, he made us do the three work sequences on page 135 with a slight pause in between. We were then encouraged to try a faster pace to gradually wipe out the pauses and come down to the prescribed three seconds.

Applied anywhere a fixed, non-jamming eye was needed, and we learnt to trust it implicitly when drawn tight in cordage with a good surface and healthy core.

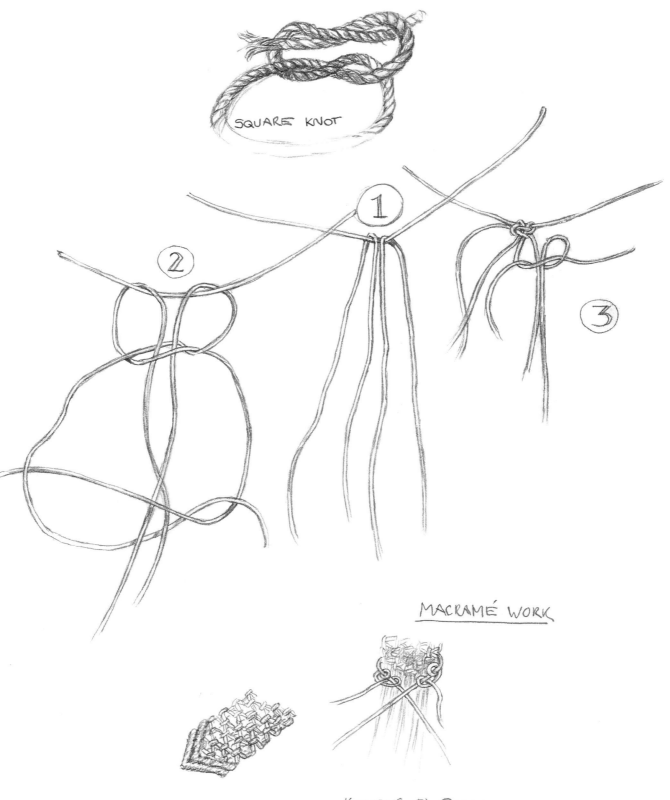

SQUARE KNOT

MACRAMÉ WORK

KNOTTING TO FINISH

137

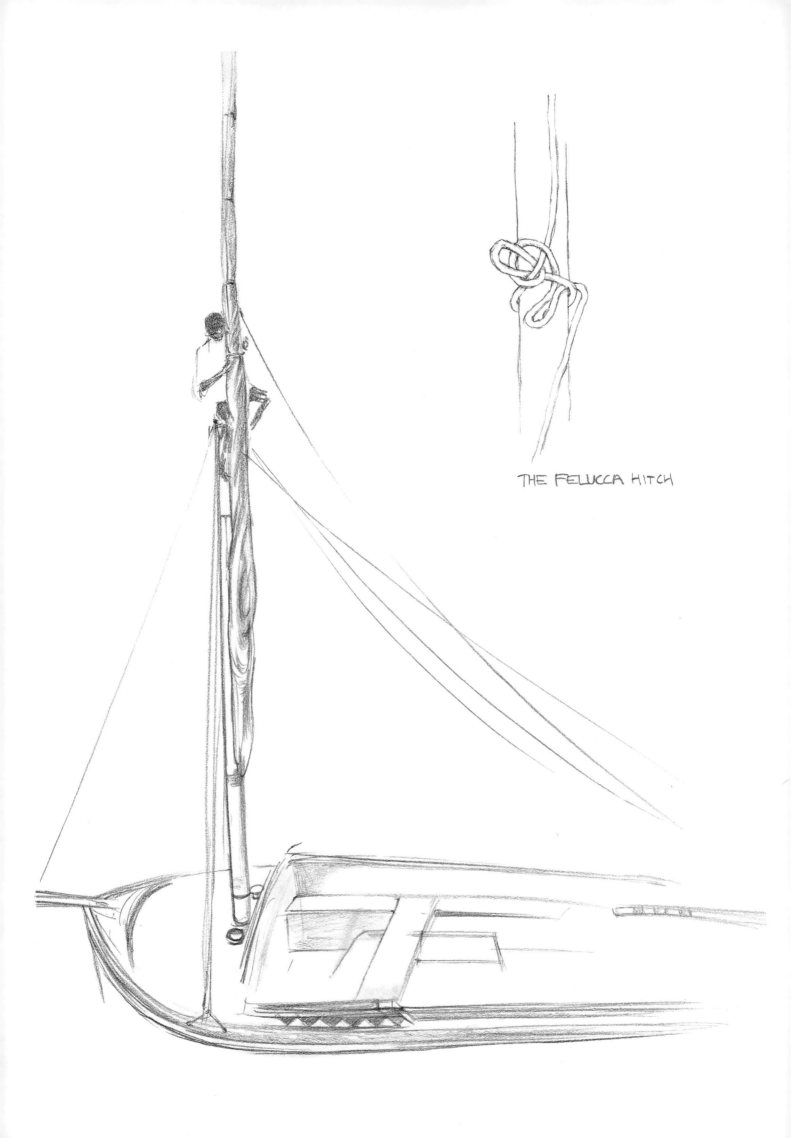

THE FELUCCA HITCH

In small stuff like cotton chalkline the square knot can be used for square knotting a handsome seagoing belt or watch strap. To make a band, add doubled twine on either side of the central knot. Square knots are continued in a diagonal pattern and the band is finished by taking the outermost, lines towards the centre as the other lines are half hitched to them in double rows.

I did not learn much more until the *Moth*'s Mediterranean sojourn. Coming through green foamy water into the Venetian harbour at Heraklion on Crete, seeking shelter from a nasty nor-easter, I dropped the close-reefed sails and found a tie-up space next to a Yugoslavian trabaccoli. A man in a dark blue sweater was leaning easily against the trabaccoli's sweeping stem.

'Salve,' I yelled.

'Salve,' he nodded.

I let go the stern anchor and the *Moth* went in. Given the high quay, the strong surge, and the shortness of my lines, it was impossible for the trabaccoli man to get the starboard line to a bollard. Instead, he deftly tied it in midair to a hawser running ashore from his own boat, raised a courteous hand and disappeared towards the municipal bus station.

Later I examined the midair knot and found it to be a faultlessly laid rolling hitch, a logical and lucid choice for the occasion.

ROLLING HITCH

On the Nile, sailing on the felucca of Akasha Falifa Mohammed Mahmud, the large cotton sails were not dropped and secured along the boom or lower spar but hoisted high and gathered with an unrecorded knot that I will call the Felucca hitch. This satisfies the given need with precision and style. You cannot help learning with pleasure the knots which are so aptly brought before you.

To conclude, I will put before you another such gift. It will stand you in good stead when you find that a halyard is coming apart.

35
A simple halyard splice

The rope-to-wire splice is often seen as tricky work best left to the professional. In its most recent and sensible form, the splice is in fact a piece of cake.

The work of carrying the halyard wire to the customary rope tail can be done in ten minutes at dockside or on board. All one needs is a sharp knife, a ball of whipping twine and some plastic tape. A small Swedish fid or a marlinspike will be a help when tucking in the strands.

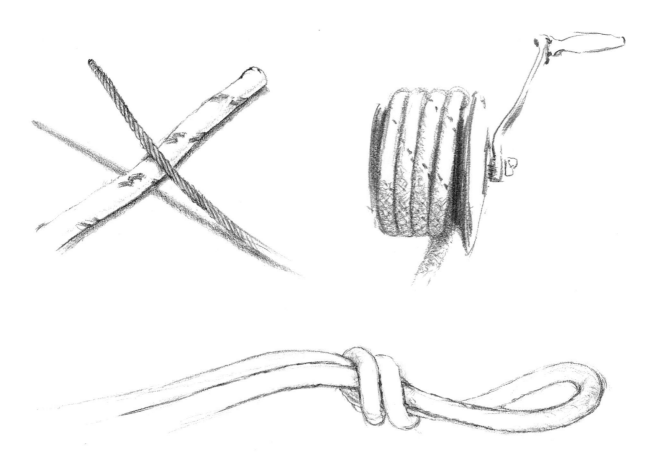

The origins of this splice go back to my visits to the Albrechtsson-Hasse rigging floor in Göteborg, Sweden, at the time when I worked upstairs in the sail loft. Ten years ago, I used a rudimentary version of it in a marlinspike book but the present, fully matured and reliable splice owes some of its finer points to Eda Mejer, a lady rigger with a quarter of a century's experience at the Selden yacht rigging plant in Göteborg. She herself ties a neat rope-to-wire splice in a few minutes, listening to popular requests on the radio and balancing a cup of black coffee on the side.

If you are replacing a worn-out splice, start by matching up 7 mm (diameter) × 19 strand wire to braided rope (6 mm wire to 12 mm rope being appropriate in a 30-footer).

Begin the splice by tying an overhand loop knot 1½ fathoms from the end of the rope braid.

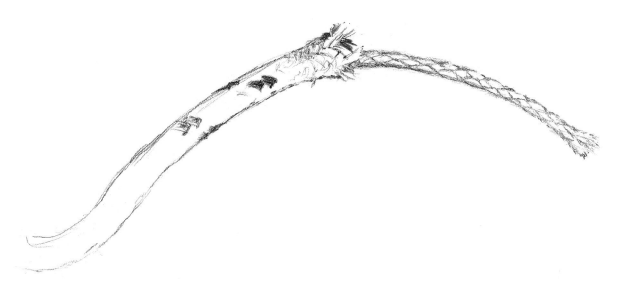

Pull out 50 cm (20 in) of the core braid and cut 15 cm (5 in) off the end.

To enter the wire into the end of the core, it is necessary to tape or serve it over the end so that the wire does not catch. I ask to have my wires heat-shrunk at the ends when buying them which blunts and points the wire ends even better. Feed the wire 40 cm (15 in) into the core.

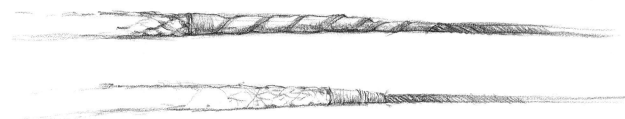

Fix the core to the wire by serving over the end with fabric-based electrician's tape. This gives a comfortable berth for a simple serving with twine (see bottom of page 142).

'Milk' the outer braid back over the core so that it takes its proper place well below (15 cm; 5 in) the end of the core.

Unravel the cover braid as far back as the serving on the wire and gather the loose ends into three strands, taping them at the end. One strand is passed under two strands of wire. I rotate the splice towards me and pass the next strand at the exit point of the previous strand, again under two wire strands. Rotating the splice towards me as the strands are passed, I work round until all three strands have been passed three times and are pulled well home every time. Cut the ends and serve over with twine on plastic tape to finish.

Lacking the full loft facilities for a final serving in the traditional style described in manuals of marlinspike seamanship, you need only make an extended whipping as shown starting at the bottom of this page.

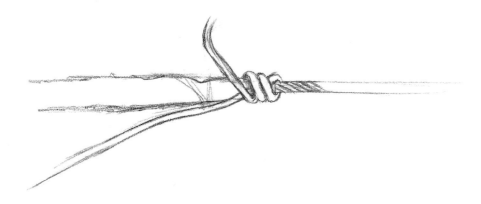

Serve the whipping twine back over itself from where the taped rope and the wire meet, as shown above. When nearly all the taped section has been covered, double back the end of the whipping twine that lies along the rope; continue to serve over with the other end of the twine until the tape is covered; poke the end of the twine up in the previously made loop and pull the loop under the last bit of serving to secure it; cut the ends close.

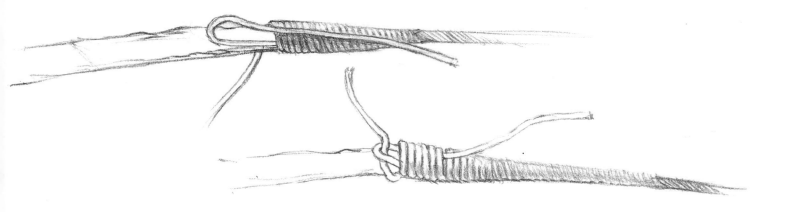

When the halyard is rigged up, the concealed wire end should be just off the halyard winch drum when the sail is hoisted with maximum luff tension. Otherwise, wear on the splice is increased.

That's it. Not very hard, was it?

PAXOS FISHERMAN'S WHIPPING